Colours
in the Dark

James Reaney

copyright © 1969 James Reaney

Talonbooks
201 1019 East Cordova
Vancouver
British Columbia V6A 1M8
Canada

This book was typeset by Linda Gilbert of B.C. Monthly
Typesetting Service, designed by David Robinson, and
printed by Gordon Fidler.

Fourth printing: July 1975

Talonplays are edited by Peter Hay.

ISBN 0-88922-001-8

Author's Note from the Original Production

Colours in the Dark might best be called a play box. Why?

I happen to have a play box and it's filled with not only toys and school relics, but also deedboxes, ancestral coffin plates — in short, a whole life. When you sort through the play box you eventually see your whole life — as well as all of life — things like Sunday School albums which show Elijah being fed by ravens, St. Stephen being stoned. The theatrical experience in front of you now is designed to give you that mosaic — that all-things-happening-at-the-same-time-galaxy-higgledy-piggledy feeling that rummaging through a play box can give you. But underneath the juxtaposition of coffin plate with baby rattle with Royal Family Scrapbook with Big Little Book with pictures of King Billy and Hitler, there is the backbone of a person growing up, leaving home, going to big cities, getting rather mixed up and then not coming home again, but making home and identity come to him wherever he is. The kids at the very end of the play manage to get their lightning rod up and attract the thunder that alone can wake the dead. Or, on the other six hands, as Buddha says, there are any number of other interpretations that fit the mosaic we're (director, writer, actors, kids, designers, composer) giving you.

For example, you can just sit back and watch the sequence of colours in the play: from a white section, to red, orange, yellow, green, blue, purple sections, finally to black and then out to white again. Watch the colours and images the way you'd watch the peacock's feather. Myriads of characters and situations bubble up. A play box should contain lots of plays — and this one has a new play before you every two minutes. It's like one of those Christmas Concerts at a country school — you can take as much as you like from it including a Santa Claus dressed up in the best parts of all the costumes seen previously. Our Santa Claus happens to be an Angel of Death.

The writing and rehearsals have been a great deal of fun — fun enjoyed when a group is working together and constantly exchanging ideas. How about that song you used to sing called "Wal I swan?" Did I send you that pack of Tarot cards? What are the words to the Little Orphan Annie song? Isn't this the way the professors throw chalk? Not only the composer, but everyone else, particularly the children who fell upon them, sneaked over to play the piano, the parlour organ, the collection of rhythm band instruments. Surely one of the things theatre could be about is the relaxed awareness that comes when you simply play — like the weasel dancing up and down to himself near the end of Act One. Life could be an endless procession of stories, an endless coloured comic strip, things to listen to and look at, a bottomless play box.

I suppose that in the Age of Dread in which we live this may seem to some foolish. I disagree. At rehearsals I have felt (and the rehearsals were in my high school auditorium with a great many teachers of mine looking down from portraits) here was such a peaceable kingdom — energetic, joyful and serene — it made the world of dread much easier to face afterwards.

So, open the lid, watch what we do with some chairs, some words and some magic lantern slides.

James Reaney
Stratford, Ontario
June and July, 1967

CAST

PA plays the Father, the Hero, the Schoolmaster, the Executive, etc.

MA plays the Mother, the Lawyer, the Announcer, the Windlady, the girl at the boarding house, the Rich Young Lady, etc.

GRAMP plays the Grandfather, the Bear, James McIntyre, the Ingersoll cheese poet, Mr. Winemeyer, Professor Button, the Angel of Death, etc.

GRAM plays the Grandmother, a Sundog, the lady who initiates the hero into a knowledge of himself, Granny Crack, the Music Teacher, the old woman who ladles out horse soup, the mistress of the Winnipeg boarding house, etc.

SON plays the Son, the Boy, the Judge, the Grocery Clerk, etc.

NIECE plays the Daughter, the Girl, Bible Sal, the Bride, etc.

Colours in the Dark was first performed at the Avon Theatre in Stratford, Ontario on July 25, 1967, with the following cast:

Pa	Douglas Rain
Ma	Martha Henry
Gramp	Sandy Webster
Gram	Barbara Bryne
Son	Heath Lamberts
Niece	Mary Hitch
Children	Jane Brooks, David Carroll
	Laurie Carroll, Lea Carroll
	Jocelyn Drainie, Elliott Hayes
	John Livingstone, Gregory Misener
	Judy Murray, Bruce Rowe
	Jim Wendland, Peter Young
Chorus	Garnet Brooks, Michael Fletcher
	Muriel Greenspoon, Elsie Sawchuk

Directed by John Hirsch
Sets by Eoin Sprott
Costumes by Don Lewis
Music by Alan Laing

Colours in the Dark was also performed at the Playhouse Theatre in Vancouver, British Columbia on December 5, 1969, with the following cast:

Pa	Eric House
Ma	Daphne Goldrick
Gramp	Walter Marsh
Gram	Barbara Tremain
Son	Glenn MacDonald
Niece	Nicola Lipman
Children	Guy Babineau, Tom Bulmer
	Sarah Fleming, Sean Flynn
	John Gates, Maisie Hoy
	Peter Vaughan, Paisley Woodward
Chorus	Colin Bernhardt, Jackie Crossland
	Rosanne Hopkins, Richard Marcuse

Directed by Timothy Bond
Sets by Brian Jackson
Costumes by Margaret Ryan
Music by Alan Laing

to J.A.R.

Act One

1. A FAMILY GAME AND A BIRTHDAY PARTY

*The houselights aren't down yet and the play
has already begun with a young man, SON,
circling around the stage on a bicycle. At the
back of the stage — projection screens show
colours. There are half-a-dozen kitchen chairs
lined up Centre Stage and as CHILDREN start
arriving on stage and the four SINGERS come
out on the other side of the stage, GRAND-
MOTHER, GRANDFATHER, FATHER,
MOTHER and NIECE arrive, the bicyclist
stops and a game of Musical Chairs starts up,
the SINGERS providing the music. Down in the
pit, pianist and drummer — the pianist probably
secretly controlling the music cues that mean
everyone must find a chair, and if they can't
they are out. For each turn a chair gets taken
away. The singers sing songs like "Big Rock
Candy Mountain" and hymns like "Shall We
Gather at the River." This Musical Chairs game*

*is a real game, during the first run no one ever
knew who was going to win and great rivalry
for Mother's prize — a balloon handed up by
the pianist — great rivalry grew up between
grown-up actors and children.*

*On one side of the stage GRANDFATHER
mends his bagpipes. On the other side GRAND-
MOTHER plays with a pack of Tarot cards. The
SON is picking a bouquet of huge paper flowers.
Now, as MOTHER speaks, the houselights begin
to go down.*

MA:

Time for one more game, Father, while I go in and
light the candles on your cake.

KIDS:

Blindfold him! *They do.* Now guess who we are.

They form a circle around him.

SON:

Make him read your palms at the same time.

KIDS:

Read our palms. Guess who we are. Read our palms.
Guess who we are.

An image of upraised hands to a bandaged face.

2. GUESSING OR THE DANCE OF LIFE

PA:

Aha! Erasmus William Wrigley. Now let's have all your hands.

In the guessing sequence there should be several attempts to fool him.

Ah — strongly and deeply entrenched bracelets. You'll be a policeman.

Oldsters crawl towards him on their knees.

Sarah Elizabeth Brody. A missing front tooth. A strong mount of Mercury. You'll be a rich young lady.

A CHILD presents him with a bare foot.

Daniel Pickett!! You'll be a postman. Ann Young. You'll be an Indian Chief! Ah! Alexander Maurice Quick. Your mind and heart lines are joined together. You'll be a Poet or a Painter.

This BOY leaves the circle, sits by himself on the single chair still remaining from the first game. GRANDFATHER, crawling forward, extends his bagpipe chanter.

You're my father. And that is not a hand — that's the left nostril of your bagpipes. You'll be an Angel of Death. Ah! Margaret Mary Cumber. A very high hill of the Moon. You'll be a dressmaker — of high fashion. And this is an —

The GRANDMOTHER presents him with one of those toy plastic Hallowe'en skeletons.

> —An odd little boy who came to school
> And lives in the cemetery
> His mother is a gravestone, his father a ghoul
> But we don't mind that very
> At mathematics he's awfully smart
> His backbone's useful to count on   *laughing*
> And I think it's because he's got no heart —
> — I can't think up anymore.

> *He is presented with a plastic Jack O'Lantern.*

Now this little chap has a candle for a mind and will grow up to be a piece of pumpkin pie.

KIDS: *dancing a Dance of Birth and singing a tune the pianist makes up.*

> A Policeman and a Rich Young Lady
> An Indian Chief and a Postman
> Poet, Skeleton, Dressmaker
> Angel of Death and Pumpkin Pie.

SON:

Now let's try father on these flowers. A flower to each child.

> *The CHILDREN are sitting in a circle reaching the flower up to him.*

PA:

To my touch — it seems red! I hear this flower — orange. I smell this flower — yellow. I touch this flower — ah, a Jack in the Pulpit! I taste this — blue.

GRAM: *interplacing one of the Tarot cards*
What is the colour of this?

PA:

It's not a flower at all. It is one of your Tarot Cards, Mother. *pause* The Fool. And what he's looking for he carries on his back. *pause* A purple flower. A white one — Ah — Sally.

NIECE proffers the Bible she is always reading.

Black. The tough hide your Bible's bound in.

MA:

And what flower is this?

Producing the cake with all its candles. He warms his hands over the candles. The stage begins to darken.

NIECE:

How did you get so good at guessing colours, Uncle?

SON:

He doesn't guess them. Father can see with his fingers.

PA:

This is a birthday cake. Mine.

He starts blowing out the candles.

Well — I'll tell you — when I was just this old — I'll tell you how I became skillful at telling — COLOURS IN THE DARK.

*The centre screen now lights up with all sorts
of colours. The cast turn to face the audience
and whisper:*

ALL:

Colours in the dark.

They blow out the candles on the cake.

3. DIALOGUE — MOTHER AND BOY SICK WITH MEASLES

*These two parts are played by the MOTHER
who brought out the birthday cake and the BOY
whose hand proclaimed him a Poet some day —
actually the scene took place years ago between
the GRANDMOTHER and the FATHER when
he was sick with the measles at about ten years
of age. The whole play is going to be like this —
six actors playing many different roles — suggest-
ing how we are many more people than just
ourselves. Our ancestors are we, our descendants
are us, and so on like a sea.*

MA:

Now. This is a cold late winter March day. While you
have the measles your room will have to be kept in
total darkness. You must not attempt to read in bed
or you will go blind. In this total darnkess you aren't
trying to read, are you?

BOY:

No, ma. I'm just holding my Planter's Peanut colouring book.

MA:

You're not also in possession of a box of crayons, too?

> *No set change here. On the bare stage the*
> *MOTHER mimes pulling down blinds. The*
> *BOY is sitting in the chair. The FATHER now*
> *begins to stand facing upstage behind the chair.*

MA:

Well — what's the use of that?

BOY:

I'm colouring in the dark. Honest, I'm not trying to
watch my hand.

MA:

What's the use of colouring in the dark?

BOY:

Because when I'm better of these measles — and you
let the light come into my room again — then I can
see if I got them anywhere near right. The COLOURS
IN THE DARK.

4. THE INITIATE — THE SUNDOGS! AND SOME QUESTIONS

> *The MOTHER, BOY and chair disappear.*
> *FATHER turns and faces us. Things begin to*
> *be lit, dim-coloured shapes appear in the dark-*
> *ness. What happens to FATHER is this: it's as*
> *if he were being initiated at a weird Masonic*
> *Lodge into an understanding of his own life.*
> *GRANDMOTHER appears as an Initiator who*
> *keeps cracking a slapstick and asking partly*

embarrassing, partly fooling questions. SON
appears with a megaphone and accuses, questions
in a very judge-like tone. The FATHER stands
in centre stage — with a figure on either side of
him. This situation recurs so often that it is like
the Sun — guarded by his two Sundogs (rainbow
scorchers) in the sky just before a storm.

FATHER, GRANDMOTHER
AND GRANDFATHER:

THE SUNDOGS

I saw the sundogs barking
On either side of the Sun
As he was making his usual will
and last testament
In a glorious vestment.
And the sundogs cried,
"Bow wow!"
We'll make a ring
around the moon
And children, seeing it, will say:
Up there they play Farmer in the Dell
And the moon like the cheese stands still.
Bow wow!
We shall drown the crickets,
Set the killdeer birds crying,
Send shingles flying,
And pick all the apples
Ripe or not.
Our barking shall overturn
Hencoops and rabbit-hutches,
Shall topple over privies
With people inside them,
And burn with invisible,
Oh, very invisible!

Flames
In each frightened tree.
Whole branches we'll bite off
And for the housewife's sloth
In not taking them in
We'll drag her sheets and pillow cases
Off the fence
And dress up in them
And wear them thin.
And people will say
Both in the country
And in the town
It falls in pails
Of iron nails.
We'll blow the curses
Right back in the farmer's mouths
As they curse our industry
And shake their fists,
For we will press the oats
Close to the ground,
Lodge the barley,
And rip open the wheat stooks.
We shall make great faces
Of dampness appear on ceilings
And blow down chimneys
Till the fire's lame.
With the noise of a thousand typewriters
We shall gallop over the roofs of town.
We are the Sun's animals.
We stand by him in the West
And ready to obey
His most auburn wish
For Rain, Wind and Storm.

*The Sundogs disappear and the GRANDMOTHER
returns as Initiator. The GRANDFATHER is
getting ready to appear in a Bear mask.*

PA:

Tell me why I can't see. Are you sundogs or are you
my left hand, my right hand, or are you my mother
and father, or are you an old beggar woman and the
old man who was the janitor at our school?

GRAM:

The reason you can't see is that you've probably
committed some crime or other. Take off your shirt
and we'll whip it out of you.

*SON strips off his Father's shirt. The would-be
initiate is scourged by the Questioner in
pantomime.*

Get the Magistrate's handbook. You must be taught
pain and joy, good and evil, life and death.

*Overtones of the Villa of the Mysteries at
Pompeii.*

*SCREEN: Faces from old family albums —
a gentleman somewhat sensual looking. On
side screens the Bosch demons attacking
St. Anthony — these change as accusations
change.*

SON: *with megaphone and book*
Have you committed —
Robbing orchards
Refusing to give half the road

Driving a Sleigh Without Bells
Travelling on Sunday with a
loaded wagon of whiskey.
Trespass, vagrancy, having arms and legs.
Being born.

> *FATHER replies "No" to all accusations.*

> *These crimes are taken from the Criminal Records for the Huron and Bruce District, 1850.*

How many horses were there in this
country in 1871?

> *FATHER answers "643,171"*

How many in 1967?

> *"552,000"*

> *Offstage the kids make hoof sounds with their fists on the floor. Diminished slightly for 1967.*

> *SCREEN: Shows the old gentleman surrounded on the side screens by 80's floozies in tights.*

SON:

Have you kept a bawdy house?
Have you ever had arms and legs?   *"No!"*
Have you ever breathed air?

GRAM:

Stop switching him. That's where the difficulty lies.
He hasn't been born yet. That's why he lives on the
sun yet can't see the earth get up.

PA:

Whose fault is that?

SON:

Yours — and a very serious crime it is too. Get
born and then we'll see.

PA:

How can I be born? Who's stopping my sun from
rising?

GRAMP: *as a bear.*

I am. I'm Grizzly Bear and I've crossed your mother's
legs and you'll never see the earth get up or the light
come down.

PA:

Blind as I am, Sundogs — I've heard you barking on
either side of me — sick the bear away where he's got
his paw over the Sun. Make him let go of my arm!

> *The Sundogs chase away the Bear. All the kids
> come yapping across the stage as dogs. Thunder!
> A bright light now fills the stage.*

5. WHITE AND DIALOGUE: BIBLE SAL

> *White suggests Sunday, Alpha, White Trillium,
> Harmonium, the Sun, "Shall we gather at the
> River," "The Big Rock Candy Mountain."*

MOTHER: *recites this.*

White is for Sunday, white trilliums, Alpha,
harmonium.

*Down in the pit the parlour organ accompanies
the four SINGERS who march across the backstage
in a row with white umbrellas singing the hymn
"Shall We Gather at the River."*

*SCREEN: A child's drawing of a trillium. The
letter A. Sunday.*

*Now we have the FATHER remembering white
things. The CHILD is colouring white things.
Back at the source of your being when your
soul gets born — clear light. Sunday afternoon.*

CENTRE SCREEN: Changes to a Green Leaf.

*NIECE enters as BIBLE SAL, a pale-faced intense
girl with a Bible.*

SON: *as a boy fishing into the orchestra pit.*
Oh, Sally, whatever is it now?

NIECE:
I just got finished copying out the book of Genesis
and I'm going ahead to copy out the whole — Bible!

SON:
You'll never do it, Sal. There isn't enough ink
and paper in this town to copy out the whole Bible.

NIECE:
I don't care if it takes all my life — I'll use my blood
for ink and my skin for paper. But I'll copy out the
whole Bible.

6. GRANNY CRACK HANGS OUT HER CLOTHES AND THE TREE BOYS FIGHT

> *GRAM plays an Old Beggar Woman who used to wander the roads of Perth County. Far back in time she remembers when our world was underneath a glacier, then it melted and coniferous trees were the first to come back. Then came the deciduous hardwoods and they're still pushing the fir trees farther and farther north.*

> *A clothesline is held up by CHILDREN and old Granny Crack comes hobbling in with her clothes.*

CHILD:

What are you doing, Granny Crack?

GRANNY:

I'm hanging up all the clothes I wear — have worn, will wear in my life. Why aren't you at Sunday School?

> *The hymn "Shall We Gather at the River" is heard in the offing.*

CHILD:

The water's too high in the flats. It's come up over the road and I can't get across to the church.

GRANNY:

All my brat and whelp clothes. Napkins and singlets and nighties.

CHILD:

What was it like here a long time ago, Granny?

GRANNY:

When I was a little girl —

CHILD:

When was that?

GRANNY:

Long before the first Indians arrived. Why the ice was piled up four miles high all over the countryside. Ice cream was cheap then, I can tell you.

"The Big Rock Candy Mountain" is heard.

CHILD:

Did you have any pets?

GRANNY:

A hairy mammoth or two. After the ice melted, the dreadful fights that took place between the trees!

SCREEN: A forest impression.

CHILD:

What about?

Two BOYS come on, one waving a fir branch, the other a maple branch. They are supported by other branch bearers.

GRANNY:

Listen.

FIR BOY:

Get out of here — you hardwood trees. Stop crowding us cone-bearers out.

MAPLE BOY:

Aw — you gummy soft wood. Now the glacier's gone, this is my territory.

FIR BOY:

Aw — your leaves drop off in the fall.

MAPLE BOY:

Take that back.

A fight between a whole company of fir branch bearers and maple branch bearers — using their branches as swords.

GRANNY:

All my dust caps. All my coats. All my galoshes.

Could the clothing wave in the wind?

There's the tear where the stones hit my back. All the hats. All the petticoats — why I used to wear seven at a time when I wandered the roads. Just to keep warm. Look where the dog tore at my stocking.

She takes off her clothes — nothing on but her shroud.

Here, hang that up, child. I've got to get into my shroud. Or get down to it.

She goes off stage throwing clothes back at the child.

CHILD:

Who won the tree battle?

Hymn should come up here.

MAPLE BOY:
>We did. Coniferous — two. Deciduous — ten!

>*A shroud comes flying in.*

CHILD:
>Just a moment, Granny, you'll need that shroud!

GRANNY: *off*
>It's all right. I've got seven shrouds on as it is —
>to keep me warm while I tramp the road to heaven.

>>*The clothesline soars up and vanishes.*
>>*The Company enter as Red Light floods the*
>>*stage.*

7. EXISTENCE POEM, RED AND THE ANCESTRAL BED

>*Red suggests Monday, BCDE, Red Zinnia,*
>*Ancestors, the Moon, a psalm, "Won't You Buy*
>*My Pretty Flowers?"*

>*This existence poem ties the whole play together*
>*and fragments of it are repeated throughout.*
>*Divide the poem for antiphony — questioner and*
>*class with FATHER as questioner.*

>>Existence gives to me
>>What does he give to me
>>He gives to me   a pebble
>>He gives to me   a dew drop
>>He gives to me   a piece of string
>>He gives to me   a straw
>>He gives to me

ALL:

Pebble   dewdrop   piece of string   straw

PA:

He gave to me — the colour RED!

NIECE:

Red as the serpent's forked tongue.

MOTHER:

Red is for Monday, red zinnias, BCDE, the Moon.

> *SCREEN: Catches all these images along with a gorgeous red panel. Then the centre panel changes to Durer's Adam & Eve. Dimly we realize that not only are we going through the hero's life and stories he heard as a child, but we are going through Canada's story — glacier and forest, also the world's story.*

PA:

The darting little tongues of the harmless garter snake.

> *A brass bed is set up.*

This story happened long before I was born.

> *Two nightshirted Ma and Pa figures appear and prepare for bed. They are played by GRAND-MOTHER and GRANDFATHER.*

MA:

Well — I've never been so tired in all my life.

PA:

That's all right, ma.

MA:

If anyone were to try to disturb me — I think I'd claw their eyes out.

PA:

I can appreciate the fact that you desire slumber, ma. Has that window been open all day?

MA:

It has. Don't you like the room airy?

PA:

I'm always afraid of that trumpet vine you planted, Evelyn. It's got right up to our bedroom window-sill this spring.

MA:

Oh shucks, Pa, stop worrying about the trumpet vine and go to sleep.

They retire back to back.

PA: *disturbed by something.*
I thought you said you wanted to sleep this night, wife.

MA:

So I did. And I do.

PA: *pause.*
Then what are you tickling my back for?

MA:

I'm not. Now shut up and go to sleep before I brain you.

PA mumbles.

MA:

What's the matter with you?

PA:

Nothing.

MA:

Put your back to me and go to sleep. That's a command.

PA:

I am. I'm not laying a hand on you. I couldn't.

MA:

You certainly are, you liar. You're tickling my back.

PA:

Look here, mother — I am not!

MA:

Oh — Samuel! Either you've changed somewhat or — there's something in the bed with us.

PA:

Great Jehovah! It must have climbed up the trumpet vine this afternoon, crawled under the covers and gone to sleep.

MA:

What for the Sweet Lord's sake.

PA:

This!

Holding up a huge undulating black snake.

MA:
> A snake!

> *Bed, snake, and GRANDPARENTS with their "ruin original" disappear screaming.*

8. "BERRY-PICKING"

MOTHER:
> The Story of the Berry-Picking Child and the Bear.

> *SCREEN: A child's drawing of a berry-picking woods.*

PA:
> This happened early near the Little Lakes.

KIDS: *darting about with berry pails*
> Look at the raspberries
> Wild Gooseberries
> Huckleberries
> Over here!
> Look at the raspberries
> Wild currants.
> Don't eat them. They're poison.
> Bunch berries (ugh!)

> *One CHILD is left busily picking. Her name is SADIE.*

GRAMP: *entering as a bear and lifting up a child*
> Child, my cubs need nurse. I need your blood.

SADIE:

> Wouldn't blood red berries do instead?

GRAMP:

> No. Flesh must be my bread.

SADIE:

> Put me down, Mr. Bear, I do thee dread.

> *Bear runs off with child, kids enter shrieking.*

KIDS:

> A bear ran off with Sadie! A bear ran off with Sadie!
> And it takes a lot of people to produce one child.

> *They form a family tree pyramid with a
> reappearing SADIE.*

KIDS:

It takes

Two parents

Four Grandparents

Eight Great Grandparents

Sixteen Great great grandparents

Thirty-two Great great great grandparents

Sixty-four Great great great great grandparents

One hundred and twenty-eight Great great great great great grandparents

Two hundred and fifty-six Great great great great great great grandparents

Five hundred and twelve Great great great great great great great grandparents

One thousand and twenty-four Great great great great great great great great grandparen

It would take over a thousand people to do this scene. At Listeners' Workshop we did it with thirty-two people. The children here suggested by a triangle arrangement, the thousand ancestors behind each human being. Have one group of players in charge of changing "Great great" & "grandparents."

SADIE:

Are you there 1,024 ancestors?

A feeble rustle

Are you there 512?
Are you there 256?
Are you there 128?

Sound gets louder, less ghost-like and more human.

Are you there 64?
Are you there 32?
Are you there 16?

More recent ancestors step forward and say firmly and clearly what we have only dimly heard: "We're here."

Are you there 8?
Are you there 4?
Are you there Mother and Father?

GRAMP, MA and PA step forward and establish the next scene as the kids fade away.

9. THE CHRISTENING

*A couple advance with a marionette baby in
their hands. A minister comes to meet them
with a basin of water and a Bible under his
arm. The couple is played by MOTHER and
FATHER, the minister by GRANDFATHER.*

REVEREND:

You've come about Christening your new baby—
Mr. and Mrs. I didn't quite catch the names on your
note — the rain had blurred it and anyhow, you
depended, evidently, on the wind to post it for you.

MR:

I can't remember my name.

MRS:

Nor I mine. What's yours?

REVEREND:

Such insomnia is extremely contagious. I can't
remember mine either. Never mind. It will come
to us when we start — what are you christening
this child?

MR:

We can't make up our minds.

REVEREND:

In a pinch you can always use the surname as a first
name. Smith Smith, you know. Or suppose the
mother's surname was White or Black. Why, simply
append it to the father's surname.

Baby flies up and off.

MR:

My goodness me, Annie, where'd our baby go?

MRS:

Just here a moment ago, Sandy.

MR:

I distinctly saw it in our arms, Elmira.

REVEREND:

Now what about a Biblical name?

Infant returns as a BOY to join his parents.

Ah, yes — a Biblical name for a boy.

MRS:

What about Abez?

MR:

What's the meaning of it though?

REVEREND:

An egg. Muddy.

A GIRL comes and the BOY and GIRL run off.

MRS:

Achizib has a good sound.

MR:

Not bad at all.

REVEREND:

It means liar, lying, one that runs.

BOY comes in older.

MR:

I know its girlish — but Beulah?

REVEREND:

It means married.

NIECE and SON enter as bride and bridegroom. BOY exits.

MRS:

And so he is. Married already. And we haven't even got him named yet.

NIECE and SON exeunt.

MR:

I know — I'll close my eyes, open up the Bible and simply stab my finger down at —

REVEREND:

Ow!

FATHER gets him in the stomach.

The FATHER and MOTHER age swiftly.

MR:

Sorry. Hold the Bible still, will you. Well — what is it?

Enter NIECE and SON with marionette baby.

THEY:

We'd like to have this baby christened.

REVEREND:

You'll have to wait your turn. It's taken us fifty years just to get a name for you. Now where is your finger and whatever your name is?

Squeezing it in the Bible.

MR:

Goodness me. You can't call a mere human being Jehovah.

MRS:

Jehovah sounds well. Jehovah Smith. He doesn't look very much like Jehovah though. I mean — where's your white beard?

The new baby flies up.

REVEREND:

That baby fly about like that very much?

SON:

Some. Not all the time. We'd better follow along with a sheet, you know, to catch him. Poor little dear — he all of a sudden forgets how to fly and down he falls with a thump!

They exit following the baby.

REVEREND:

If he stays up much longer I can think of just the right name for him. And fits in so nicely if we call you Jehovah.

SON:

A little more this way. The wind's a bit strong for him today.

REVEREND:

If he comes down — we'll call him Icarus.

MRS:

I'm very proud of my grandchild.

> *As they leave, the MOTHER gives her rocking chair a push that leaves it rocking for some time.*

REVEREND:

And if he stays up — there's nothing for it. I know this will shock you, but they do this all the time in Mexico. The only name for a child who can fly like that is —

> *Exit.*

> *SINGER enters singing a hymn about Jesus so that "Jesus" is the name he means.*

> *The Bear enters, lies down. SADIE enters, lies down on top of him and is covered by his fur coat.*

SADIE: *her voice*

And still — I got eat up by a bear. Mother! Father! Chase the bear away!

> *MOTHER AND FATHER in huge mother-and-father-carnival heads come on like marionettes. FATHER slices the Bear open. Out springs the devoured child. MOTHER sews the Bear up.*

SADIE:

Oh — thank you Father and Mother — for giving me life.

BEAR:

What about me? What am I to eat then?

SADIE:

Here, have my pail of berries

The Bear ambles off.

10. A SET OF DISHES AND BIBLE SAL AGAIN

PA:

Once one of my great grandparents bought a set of
dishes and gave it to her daughter. Slowly, down
through the years, the set of dishes grew older and
was passed on — from mother to daughter and
that daughter's daughter in turn.

*SCREEN: As we hear the history of the set
of dishes, children's drawings follow along.
"Only this cup left" is a photo of a cup. The
SON has the CHILDREN around him and with
rhythm band instruments they make breaking
and cracking sounds.*

PA:

In 1879 a saucer broke
In 1881 a cup cracked
In 1899 a handle came off a cup
In 1905 a plate was lost after a church supper
In 1920 someone got a meat platter broken over
    his head
In 1939 a kid got the soup tureen wedged on its
    head and in —
Now there's only this cup left.

BIBLE SAL appears with a huge Bible.
Green Leaf on centre screen.

SON: *fishes into orchestra pit again*
How far have you got in copying out the Bible now,
Sally?

BIBLE SAL:

Oh — far enough. The story of Onan. Oh dear.
The story of the Matron at Gibeah exposed to avoid
worse rape. They tore her in twelve pieces afterward.

SON:

Oh you wrote dirty there, Sal.

BIBLE SAL:

But I'm copying out the whole Bible and anyway
it's God who wrote it.

The school scene has been set up.

11. THE SCHOOLMASTER AND TECUMSEH

CHILDREN come in with chairs and sit down.
FATHER enters as Schoolmaster, with a switch.

SCREEN: Images of inside and outside one-room
country schools. Others red to match the school-
master's temper.

SCHOOLMASTER:

All right, we'll soon see if this class has any brains or
not. Spell — Scissors!

KID:

    S C I S O R S

SCHOOLMASTER:
    Wrong! You'll be whipped.

KID:

    S S I Z O R Z

SCHOOLMASTER:
    You'll be whipped sir!

KID:

    S C I S K N I F E

SCHOOLMASTER:
    And you'll be whipped. Next!

KID:

    S C I – S – S – O – R –– S

SCHOOLMASTER:
    Right! But I'll whip you anyhow.

    *A whipping scene where his cane eventually
    breaks on a small girl's heel.*

    Susannah! Your heel broke my cane! How dare you
    break my switch with your hard little heel!

    *We dissolve by rearranging chairs and CHILD-
    REN slowly getting up from the floor where
    they've been whipped by the Schoolmaster —
    to a trial scene in which the Schoolmaster is
    being tried for over-severe punishment.
    Schoolmaster stands Stage Right, a*

Lawyer in a gown appears to cross-examine
the Boy who, in the beginning, had his heart
and mind line joined together on his right hand.
The Laywer is played by MOTHER. She snatches
the Bible from BIBLE SAL. SON plays the Judge.

LAWYER:
Young woman, give me that Bible. I want to swear
this child in. See if the little imp is telling the truth.

The CHILDREN are testifying against the
Schoolmaster's cruelty.

You swear that the evidence we shall give between
our sovereign lord the Queen and the prisoner at
the bar shall be the truth, the whole truth and
nothing but the truth, so help you God?

KID:
So help me God!

LAWYER:
Now — kiss the Bible. Don't kiss your thumb — kiss
the Bible.

KID:
Please, sir. It's so dirty.

He kisses the Bible.

LAWYER:
You'll be put in prison and fed nothing except a crust
of bread and a cup of water — if you lie.

KID:
Yes.

LAWYER:

    Very well, Master Simeon Brinkman — did the school-master over there give you a hard licking?

KID:

    Yes. He did. Look at the red welts on my back.

LAWYER:

    Pull that shirt down. Now, Master Simeon Brinkman — did the schoolmaster over there — think carefully, and remember what I said about lying — did he give you a severe licking?

KID: *pause*

    No.

        Laughter from court.

LAWYER:

    Next witness. Miss Marybelle Cupford.

KID:

    I don't know what "severe" means.

JUDGE:

    Silence!

SCHOOLMASTER: *to audience*

    And I got off. I went out West and became Minister of Health in the first Alberta Government, Conservative Party, 1905.

      SCREEN: A Daguerrotype face — self-satisfied bearded old tyrant.

KIDS:

Hold him down! Call the Sundogs! Call Mother!
Call Father! Hold them down — Teacher, Lawyer,
Judge. You've whipped us once too often.

> *SCREEN: Faces of older actors in agony. On
> stage we see the Judge and the Lawyer crawling
> away to the sound of whips, although no actual
> whipping takes place.*

OLDER PEOPLE:

Mercy !

> *As the CHILDREN prepare to whip their
> seniors, the music suddenly introduces a
> conventional tom-tom theme.*

TECUMSEH: *played by GRAMP*

Stop! These whips are made of my skin which the
Yankees flayed from my back when I was killed
long ago with a Kentuckyman's rifle at the battle
of Moraviantown.

> *SCREEN: Change to kid's drawing of Indian
> camp.*

KID:

The battle of Moraviantown took place October 5,
1813.

> *Tecumseh extends his hands upwards.*

KIDS:

Tecumseh — are you going to die?

44

TECUMSEH:

> Help me — if I can but crawl into that hollow log over there.

> *A long cardboard box.*

> My mother was the moon, my father the sun.

> *The CHILDREN help him crawl into a hollow log. Out of the other end they pull a tortoise.*

TECUMSEH: *recorded*

> I am Tecumseh. I have changed into the tortoise who will never die. Climb on my back and I'll take you down the great river to meet your ancestors who came across the ocean in boats with white wings named.

12. SAILBOATS THAT BROUGHT ANCESTORS & A CRADLE

> *Two CHILDREN stretch a piece of blue cheese-cloth across the stage. CHILDREN with crude model sailboats slowly sail them towards us behind and above the cheesecloth sea. Standing on the chairs, six actors chant, sing solo & in unison the names of ships. Sea chanty in the background. Our ancestors in white winged vessels come closer and closer. Here are the names of their boats:*

ALL:

> Agamemnon   Kingfisher
> Alice Cooper   Lively
> Amazon   Lizzie
> Annie Bengway   Mabel Taylor

Arabia
Balaclava
Bessie Parker
Beulah
Birnam Wood
British Lion
Caleb Grimshaw
Cedar Grove
Charlotte Gladstone
City of Glasgow
Covenanter
Dancing Feather
Diadem
Early Morn
Essence of Peppermint
Eva Lynch
Flying Foam
Gypsy Bride
Go Ask Her
Glad Tidings
Hard Times
Indian Chief

Martin Luther
Parsee Merchant
Pied Nez
Queen of the North
Queen of the Seas
Quorn
Rock City
Rock Light
Royal William
Shooting Star
St. Joseph
Tea Taster
Tory's Wife
Typhoon
Ultonia
Venus
War Cloud
White Wings
Witch of the Wind
Yorkton
Zeno
Zoboah

*SCREEN: Pictures of boats, immigrants on
board ship waiting for the new country.
A cradle is brought in front of the gauze sea,
which begins to fade away. The family tree
pyramid focuses on the cradle. The six actors
stand around it variously, as ancestors, saying
to an invisible child:*

ANCESTORS:

Child — we bring across the wide sea through
the storms and the nights — your eyes.
I bring you the eye
I bring you a tooth

I bring you your left hand
I bring you the colour of your hair
I bring you your bad temper
I bring you your mind
I bring you your heart
I bring you your guts

*FATHER now leads them in some more of the
existence poem.*

The pebble is a huge dark hill I must climb
The dewdrop is a great storm that we must cross
The string is a road that I cannot find
The straw is a sign whose meaning I forget

Hill   Lake   Road   Sign

PA:

Red meets yellow and turns to orange.

13. ORANGE AND A PARADE AND A VISIT

*Orange suggests Tuesday, FGHI, Orange Lily,
Mercury, "Beulah Land," "Lillibullero."*

MA:

Orange is for Tuesday, Orange Lilies,
FGHI, Mercury.

*SCREEN: Matches what the MOTHER says:
astrological symbol for the ruling planet, then
as the Orange Parade starts, it changes to a shot
of Stratford, Ontario's main street. Then Orange
Lodge worthies. The actors, the entire Company
come on in Orange Lodge costumes, beating*

*drums, bearing King Billy banners, singing
"Lillibullero," suddenly facing us and reciting
either solo or in various combinations, the
following poem:*

FATHER, MOTHER,
GRANDFATHER AND
GRANDMOTHER:
ORANGE LILIES

On the twelfth day of July
King William will ride by
On a white horse
On a white charger
King William and Queen Mary.

He bears an orange lily
  In his hand
  (He in front
  And she behind,
  On a white horse
  On a white charger)
And so does she
On a white horse.

They're riding to see
And to jump the Boyne
  With a white horse
  In their groin,

On the twelfth day of July
King William will ride by
  With a white horse
King William and Queen Mary.

SCREEN: Suddenly projects a Union Jack.

*The Company turns its back on us, the Orange
Lodge Banners have now become Union Jacks*

and we are at the railway station waiting for
the Royal Train to pass by. With their feet the
actors pound out the rhythm of a steam engine.
Girls and boys wave Union Jacks and everyone
is singing "God Save The King," louder and
louder until — here! — the Royal Train, but it
goes right by at tremendous speed and every-
one, flags, etc., droop. A BOY turns and recites
an actual letter:

BOY:

Dear Daddy,

Our school went up June 6th to see the King and
Queen. The Royal Train was an hour late and when
the Royal Train whizzed by the school children at
10 miles an hour (it was only supposed to go 3 miles
an hour) the Royal couple weren't on the observation
platform as they should have been. They did not appear
till they had gone by 17,000 disappointed school
children. Incidentally, the Shakespeare school kids
didn't see them for they were at Stratford, but if
they had stayed at home in Shakespeare they would
have seen the King and Queen for they appeared there.
There are a lot of other newspaper clippings which
will tell you more about the mishap. If we get a chance
we will send you the Beacon with the pictures of the
Royal Visit at Stratford, published on Wednesday. It
had some excellent pictures in it. The teacher went
down the next day to see the King and Queen at
London. Everything is growing bright and green out
here. There was a heavy rain on Wednesday and I got
drenched in it coming home from music.

Our baseball team is playing the Brocksden
school team on Thursday. The five little ducks are
getting along quite fine now too, so as I'm growing
tired I'll sign off—

Your Son,

And I didn't see the King and Queen.
I can't get over it!

*Our attention now swerves to FATHER who
stands on a slowly emptying stage and recites a
poem that was written six years after the letter:*

PA:

THE ROYAL VISIT

When the King and Queen came to Scotland
Everyone felt at once
How heavy the Crown must be.
The Mayor shook hands with their Majesties
And everyone presentable was presented
And those who weren't resented
It, and will
To their dying day.
Everyone had almost a religious experience
When the King and Queen came to visit us
(I wonder what they felt!)
And hydrants flowed water in the gutters
All day.
People put quarters on the railroad tracks
So as to get squashed by the Royal Train
And some people up the line at Shakespeare
Stayed in Shakespeare, just in case —
They did stop too,
While thousands in Stratford

Didn't even see them
Because the Engineer didn't slow down
Enough in time
And although,
But although we didn't see then in any way
(I didn't even catch the glimpse
The teacher who was taller did
Of a gracious pink figure)
I'll remember it to my dying day.

Now — let's have some religious dispute.

SCREEN: A reprise of the Royalist and Orange images.

14. BAITING

Like the fighting between the coniferous and deciduous trees — the CHILDREN break up into two groups who bait each other. Two lines of CHILDREN lean out against each other. The four SINGERS in Salvation Army hats line up on Stage Left.

CATHOLIC KIDS:
Protestant, Protestant, quack, quack, quack
Go to the devil and never come back.

PROTESTANT KIDS:
The Catholic brats, they don't like cats.
They don't eat meat on Friday.

CATHOLIC KIDS:
The Pope he is a gentleman
He wears a watch and chain;

King Billy is a beggarman
And lives in a dirty lane.

PROTESTANT KIDS:
King Billy is a gentleman
He wears a watch and chain;
The Pope he is a beggarman
And lives in a dirty lane.

> *They start to tussle, but are interrupted by the*
> *hymn "Beulah Land" from the SINGERS. They*
> *all turn on them instead, taunt them and run*
> *off.*

ALL:
The Salvation Army, free from sin,
Went to heaven in a cornbeef tin.

> *The SINGERS, shaking their tambourines, also*
> *vanish and there is a moment of — nothing.*
> *Perhaps the light on the bare stage changes a*
> *bit. SCREEN is empty, and then:*

15. LITTLE ORPHAN ANNIE

> *A small GIRL comes on in a pink frilly Shirley*
> *Temple dress with Orphan Annie eyes and tap*
> *dances to the Orphan Annie theme song once*
> *heard every night just before supper time on*
> *the radio. The SINGERS dance across the*
> *stage before singing the song.*

SINGERS:

>Who's that little chatterbox
>The one with curly auburn locks?
>You really want to know?
>It's little Orphan Annie.
>
>Mite size, cheeks a rosy glow
>She's a source of healthiness handy
>Bright eyes always on the go
>Arf, says Sandy and
>
>Who's that little chatterbox
>The one with curly auburn locks?
>You really want to know?
>It's little Orphan Annie.

>*SCREEN: Thirties — radio figures and adver-
>tising material. That kind of lettering they use
>in the New York Automat.*

16. THE WALKERS

*This sequence is about beginning to wonder
where you've come from; then beginning to
wonder where you go. FATHER and SON
here play young boys just about twelve.*

PA: *coming up with a folded handkerchief*
>Hey! What's this! Bet you don't know.

SON:
>No, I don't.

PA:
>It's a woman.

SCREEN: The roads of Perth County. White gravel roads running by fences, woodlots, villages.

PA:

First you swam in your father's groin
Then you hang from a mother tree
Up from the groundhog's den you join
The baby animals' crawling spree.

GRAM:

Watch people walking.

PA:

I watched from the gate way — her walking towards me.

GRAM as the Old Beggar Woman, Granny Crack, mimes walking down a road. She sings "Beulah Land." GRAMP dressed as an Old Tramp, now goes by in the opposite direction singing "The Big Rock Candy Mountain."

PA:

I watched him go by.

The Tramp supports himself with two canes and has a huge sack on his back. The Tramp and the Beggar Woman now converge on FATHER and with him recite the following poem about the wandering Granny Crack.

GRAM:

I was a leather skinned harridan
I wandered the county's roads
Trading and begging and fighting
With the sun for hat and the road for shoes.

KIDS:

>You played a pigsty Venus
>When you were young, old dame,
>In the graveyard or behind the tavern
>The burdock girl was your name.

ADULTS:

>She talked vilely it is remembered,
>Was a moving and walking dictionary
>Of slang and unconventional language
>The detail of her insults was extraordinary.

GRAM:

>You saw me freckled and spotted
>My face like a killdeer's egg
>When, berry-picking kids, you ran from me
>Frightened down the lane by the wood.

ALL:

>They saw her as an incredible crone
>The spirit of neglected fence corners,
>Of the curious wisdom of brambles
>And weeds, of ruts, of stumps and of things despised.

GRAMP:

Put your hands over your ears you can hear your feet
walking beneath you. Crunch — Crunch.

GRAM:

Put your hands over your feet — you can feel your
breath walking — one breath in, one breath out.

ALL:

Look at the world upside down.

Looking at the audience through their legs.

ALL:

It's much clearer that way. The bottom part of your eyes would also like to look at some sky.

PA:

I used to walk in the winter.

A white sheet is carried by.

I used to walk in the summer.

A green sheet is carried by in the opposite direction. A Bagpiper comes across playing.

I passed him. He was playing at a township picnic.

An Old Fiddler crosses playing.

And I passed by him I almost forgot. Once at a party — I saw four old men in a jig contest.

Cast members somehow manage this. Then FATHER sits down and mimes watching a leaping, dancing weasel.

I saw dancing by himself in the grass by the road — a weasel.

Granny Crack returns and says:

GRAM:

I was the mother of your sun
I was the sister of your moon
My veins are your paths and roads
On my head I bear steeples and turrets
I am the darling of your god.

17. THE WHEEL — A TRIP UP TOWN

Out of two trestles — sawhorses — make a cart.
A buggy. Cocoanut shells for horses' hooves.
Have FATHER announce that it is a trip up
town and he, with GRAM and GRAMP as
driver, climb into the buggy. FATHER starts
the following poem but it gets passed around
to the other two in the buggy:

The red buggy wheels move so fast
   They stand still
Whirling against sheaves of blue chicory
The secret place where wild bees nest
The million leaning pens of grass with their
                        nibs of seed,
   The wild rose bush — all
   Suddenly gone.
On gravel now where corduroy logs from
                    the past
   Look dumbly up.
Buried in the congregations of gravel,
   Getting closer the highway
   Cars darting back and forth
   In another world altogether
Past the stonemason's house with its
                  cement lion
Not something to be very much afraid of
   Since it has legs like a table,
Past the ten huge willows, the four poplars,
   Far away in a field the slaughterhouse,
   Two gas stations with windy signs.
The half world of the city outskirts; orchards
Gone wild and drowned farms.
   Suddenly the square —
People turning and shining like lighted jewels,

Terrifying sights: One's first nun!
The first person with a wooden leg,
The huge chimney writing the sky
With dark smoke.
A parrot.
A clock in the shape of a man with its face
In his belly
The swan
A dixie-cup of ice cream with a wooden spoon.

18. A VISIT TO A STORE

*SCREEN: The interior of a 1910 general store.
The main paraphernalia is some sort of counter
with, above it, a ball of string that feeds into a
hook or hole on the counter. The Grocer, the
Clerk, the Lady Customer. The Grocer is very
grocery — straw cuffs to protect his shirt cuffs.
The Clerk is adolescent — the essence of the
breed. It's best to play this with invisible string.
The Clerk wraps up the Lady's parcel. Ties it —
but does not break the string. The Lady walks
out of the store, the string still attached to her
parcel. She walks into the audience. FATHER
plays the Grocer and SON plays the Clerk.*

GROCER:
Cut the string?

He turns from some task.

CLERK: *hesitating*
Not yet. *feebly* Hey! Lady!

GROCER:
Cut the string!

CLERK: *hovering with scissors*
I can't. It's got me mesmerized.

GROCER:
Here — give me those scissors. Oh — I can't cut it either. It's too — do you suppose she'll use up a whole ball of string?

They watch the revolving ball.

19. ODE ON THE MAMMOTH CHEESE

In front of the grocery skit GRAMP comes rolling a huge orange medicine ball. Or GRAM rolls it in for him.

GRAMP:
Besides being a grandfather, a janitor at the school, and a bagpipe player, I was also an undertaker at Beachville where I found something to sing about.

GRAM:
The biggest cheese the world has ever seen!

GRAM:
ODE ON THE MAMMOTH CHEESE
— by James McIntyre

Piano and drums build and build

Weight over seven thousand pounds.

We have seen thee, queen of cheese,
Lying quietly at your ease
Gently fanned by evening breeze
Thy fair form no flies dare seize.

All gaily dressed soon you'll go
To the great Provincial show
To be admired by many a beau
In the city of Toronto.

Cows numerous as a swarm of bees,
Or as the leaves upon the trees
It did require to make thee please
And stand unrivalled, queen of cheese,

May you not receive a scar as
We have heard that Mr. Harris
Intends to send you off as far as
The world's great show at Paris.

Of the youth beware of these,
For some of them might rudely squeeze
And bite your cheek, then songs or glees
We could not sing, oh! the queen of cheese.

Wert thou suspended from balloon
You'd cast a shade even at noon,
Folks would think it was the moon
About to fall and crush them soon.

GRAMP:

Just one moment — I've got some other recitations
here. Lines on a Typewriter? Lines on a Lawn Party?
Walt Whitman? Night Blooming Cereus . . .

They bandage his mouth and drag him off.

20. STRING

We fade back to the string story.

GROCER:
> Great Thundering Jupiter! She hasn't got home yet, where does she live — that's a mile of string we've given her . . .

CLERK: *with an armful*
> Put on another ball of string?

GROCER:
> No — she's not going to ruin me by running up my string bill. No — wind her back.

> *Have this a big comic grotesque moment as they wind back the string — pull the lady and her parcel up out of the audience, down the aisle, onto the stage — but when they wind her back the first time they get a skeleton lady holding the parcel.*

CLERK:
> What did we do wrong that time?

GROCER:
> Uh — you wound her back too slow. You got behind time and she died on us. Let her go — and we'll pull her back faster this time. See what we get.

Various helpers with the string are yanked
offstage as the skeleton lady runs away with the
string. Now a tug of war develops. They pull —
she and her helpers pull — finally they get the
string running again — this time the Grocer
and his Clerk pull like mad and in comes,
carrying the identical parcel, a small girl.

CLERK:
What'd we do wrong that time?

GROCER: *out of breath*
We pulled too fast. Let her go. Shoo little girl.
Don't come back till you're old enough to buy that
parcel.

Their routine dims out — implying that it will
go on forever.

21. THE BRIDGE — OR EVEN ADOLF HITLER HAD 1024 GREAT GREAT GREAT GREAT GREAT GREAT GREAT GREAT GRANDPARENTS AND KEPT A PLAY BOX TOO

FATHER speaks, SON acts out situation for him.

PA:
On one of my walks — I came to a river. There was a
bridge. But under the bridge there was a swan. He
hissed at me. I couldn't cross.

Set this up as a bridge with something white
under it. A girl with a long white glove as the
swan's neck. The situation — the entire Company
crosses the bridge, but the hero can't. On the

other side they beckon to him silently, but he won't cross.

PA:

I can't cross. I'm afraid! I was like one of those people you hear about in mental hospitals who can't go through a doorway.

The pebble is a huge dark hill I must climb
The dewdrop is a great storm lake that we must cross
The string is a road that I cannot find
The straw is a sign whose meaning I forget

Hill   Lake   Road   Sign

The Bear chases him to the middle of the bridge. A tug of war between the people and the Bear helped by Lady Death. He is pulled across — perhaps loses something. The Bear and Lady Death dispute over this — with some other sinister figures who gather. Lady Death is played by GRANDMOTHER. They fade and the cast from the family tree pyramid; the Stage turns slowly yellow.

ALL:

It Takes
The Remembering
Of   four   seasons
Eight   Stars
Sixteen   Sunsets
Thirty-two   Wind whistles
Sixty-four   Dewdrops in the sunrise
One hundred and twenty-eight Trembling leaves
Two hundred and fifty-six   Pebbles
Five hundred and twelve   Snowflakes
One thousand and twenty-four   Cloud shadows
To make one soul

The family tree pyramid now reverses so it is an arrow pointing at a child standing on the trestles. This child turns his face. He is masked and dressed as Adolf Hitler.

SCREEN: Swastika

We hear a Nazi children's song and the roar of a Nuremberg rally. All file off, FATHER helping the Hitler boy down and off.

Act Two

1. YELLOW AND ANTICHRIST AS A CHILD

*Yellow suggests Wednesday, JKLM, Sunflower,
Swallowtail Butterfly, Venus, Beckwith's
"Hymn," Mendelssohn's "On Wings of Song."*

MOTHER:
Yellow is for Wednesday, swallowtail butterfly,
JKLM, the planet Venus.

*SON enters, sits down and plays the spokes of
his bike. The Hitler boy appears with FATHER,
who turns to the audience and recites:*

FATHER:
ANTICHRIST AS A CHILD

When Antichrist was a child
He caught himself tracing
The capital letter A
On a window sill

And wondered why
Because his name contained no A.
And as he crookedly stood
In his mother's flower-garden
He wondered why she looked so sadly
Out of an upstairs window at him.
He wondered why his father stared so
Whenever he saw his little son
Walking in his soot-coloured suit.
He wondered why the flowers
And even the ugliest weeds
Avoided his fingers and his touch.
And when his shoes began to hurt
Because his feet were becoming hooves
He did not let on to anyone
For fear they would shoot him for a monster.
He wondered why he more and more
Dreamed of eclipses of the sun,
Of sunsets, ruined towns and zeppelins,
And especially inverted, upside down churches.

*As he finishes the poem he takes the Hitler mask
from the Kid, who slips off and goes over to a
boy who has turned his bicycle upside down and
is playing the spokes with a stick.*

66

2. THE WIND AND THE RAIN
AND A VISIT TO A SCULPTOR HERMIT

*A dancer dressed like the Wind whirls about
with a Doll dressed as the Rain. The Wind
carries her Rain Doll across the sky. FATHER
and SON play two boys on a bicycle trip. SON
is BOY 1, FATHER is BOY 2.*

BOY 1:

What're you doing?

BOY 2:

What you see me doing. What're you dressed up like
that for?

BOY 1:

Cadets. What are you thinking about then?

BOY 2:

I'm thinking about them.

*The woman in grey clothes, holding a blue rag
doll. Some projection of branch shadows as if
the Windlady walks over the trees.*

BOY 1:

Who are them?

Footlight spot and a branch-holding person.

BOY 2:

The wind and the rain.

BOY 1:

Gee — it's lucky we brought the umbrellas.

They put them up.

*SCREEN: A small, weather-beaten cottage
appears.*

BOY 2:
Aren't you afraid to knock?

We hear the Hermit playing his parlour organ.

BOY 1:
No — he's only an old hermit. He wouldn't harm you.

*He knocks on the door. A voice says: "Come in"
rather scarily. GRAMP has entered, sits on a
chair with his back to them, playing an invisible
organ. As the Hermit, he wears a straw hat,
suspenders: he slacks his body line into that
appearance a solitary often has — of a body and
face not often touched*

HERMIT:
I'm glad you've come to see me, boys. I was just
about to do my daily stint at the old pipe organ here.

He plays "On Wings of Song" — a passage or two.

Anything new in town?

BOY 2:
No. Nothing seems to happen in town. We always
feel, Mr. Winemeyer, that it all happens out here.

HERMIT:
You're right. It does. For example — On Thursday,
my barn, struck by lightning, burnt down.

BOY 2:

> I know. We saw the glow in the sky. What are you going to do for a barn, Mr. Winemeyer?

HERMIT:

> Oh, I'm rebuilding.

BOY 1:

> All by yourself?

HERMIT:

> Sure. I've always liked heights. And if you know your trigonometry, there's nothing you can't do with a couple of pulleys.

BOY 2:

> What else has happened?

HERMIT:

> Do you know what happened to me last Friday?

BOY 1:

> No. What happened to you last Friday, Mr. Winemeyer?

HERMIT:

> I died!

BOY 2:

> You what!

HERMIT:

> I died. But I rose again.

BOY 1:

> Were you buried?

HERMIT:

>Heavens no! You can't both die and bury yourself.
>Unless you arrange it all beforehand. *pause.* I rose
>on Saturday afternoon. Can't quite seem to make it
>to Sunday morning.

BOY 1:

>What else have you been up to?

HERMIT:

>Well — don't you think that's enough for one weekend?

BOY 2:

>Tell us something that happened to you when you
>were small, Mr. Winemeyer.

HERMIT:

>When I was not so small. Halfway a man. No more a
>boy. Could still see my toes. I can tell you I lived
>miles away from here in the biggest house in a stone
>town where my father was a banker. He charged
>twelve percent, sometimes twice that much. I had
>this friend of mine — the doctor's son, the minister's
>son — somebody like that — the other professional
>man's boy in a small place like that. Now you play
>me *to BOY 1* and you play him *to BOY 2* because
>you're about the right ages and I'll whisper you the
>idea of what your parts are.

>*Whispers to them.*

>*A play within a play and dimly we remember
>that a man is both his father and his son;
>everyone is a multiple character.*

3. THE STORY OF A PECULIAR KIND OF SOUP

> *SCREEN: Shows flies, horse, marsh, farmhouse images to suit.*

MOTHER:

> The story of a peculiar kind of soup.

BOY 1:

> Am I potentially homosexual?

HERMIT:

> What afloomistical? Heavens no. Just David and
> Jonathan.

BOY 1:

> Well the situation is this. Church has just finished in
> one of the many churches in this very few town and
> we're walking out to a place where a girl friend of
> both of ours has invited us to have Sunday dinner,
> right?

BOY 2:

> Only she won't appear. Because she's just had a baby
> and is lying resting upstairs. Married to some other
> type we don't think very much of. Hey! Get the
> dinner scene ready over there! *to other members of
> the cast* Now we get talking.

BOY 1:

> What have you been up to all this past year, Jacob?
> The place hasn't been the same without you.

> *SCREEN: Shows country road.*

> *The actors pretend to walk, but stay in the
> same place.*

BOY 2:

> Oh — you know what law clerks are. Even in a small city.

BOY 1:

> No — I don't even know what they're like in a small city.

BOY 2:

> I suppose. I didn't realize how sleepy life was here till I came back this Saturday. You can tell just by the sound of the minister's voice.

BOY 1:

> Well — how can that be? How does your minister's voice sound in Toronto?

BOY 2:

> I don't know. You see, I've stopped going to church.

> *SCREEN: Shows a country church.*

BOY 1:

> Jake, you haven't.

BOY 2:

> I have. And don't tell me I'm going to Hell, because I'm not and I don't believe there is such a place.

BOY 1:

> Now look here. You shouldn't criticize good things like that.

BOY 2:

> Good things! There's another superstition I'm going
> to rid you of too. I suppose you still think it's wrong
> to go to bed with a woman unless you're married to
> her.

BOY 1:

> Yes, I do.

BOY 2:

> Well I'm not married. And I have.

BOY 1:

> Go on. You're lying.

BOY 2:

> I am not.

BOY 1:

> I'll bet. Once maybe.

BOY 2:

> Lots of times. And with different women.

BOY 1:

> After this — I'm quiet and don't say much. And then
> we come to the house. It's away out in the country
> on a farm beside the marsh. I remember he went up
> to talk to our friend who was still kept to her room
> after having a baby. I stayed downstairs. Even
> though they had a well-filled fly sticker and a much-
> used fly swatter, they still had a lot of trouble with
> flies in that house.

> *GRAM can be the farmwife here. NIECE stands
> to one side combing her hair. The handing out*

of soup at a table is mimed. BOY 1 refusing to
have any. Then the other BOY appears, is
offered soup and accepts. He is watched
curiously by the others.

BOY 2:
>Then I asked what kind of soup it was.

GRAM: *ladling him out some more*
>If you like it put into it.

>*She ladles him out more.*

BOY 1:
>Then we took leave of that family. We didn't like the
>boy who had married our friend, and it was his father's
>place we were at. We were walking back across the
>flat marsh country changing with cloud shadows.

BOY 2:
>Are you still angry with me?

BOY 1:
>Know what you just had for dinner?

BOY 2:
>Yes. Boiled beef and potatoes. And that soup she
>served.

BOY 1:
>Have you ever had horsemeat before?

BOY 2:
>No.

BOY 1:

> They butchered a horse yesterday. That was what
> the soup was — and the meat — likely.

BOY 2: *pause*

> Why didn't you tell me?

BOY 1:

> That it was horse soup? I thought you'd know since
> you've gone away to law school and become so smart
> and had so much experience.

> *BOY 2 mimes vomiting.*

BOY 2:

> Oh you fool. It was all a lie. Things like that are
> mostly lies. It was a lie.

> *BOY 1 and Hermit speak together.*

BOY 1:

> It's not a lie now, is it. It's not a lie now.

HERMIT:

> And I said: It's not a lie now, is it. It's not a lie now.

> *He holds a peacock feather.*

BOY 1:

> Where'd you get the peacock feather, Mr. Winemeyer?

HERMIT:

> Had a pet peacock once when I was a boy. A big old
> sow we had had a peeve about it — and one day caught
> it in the orchard and devoured it. This — was all
> that was left of my beautiful bird. Sticking out of
> that beast's mouth.

BOY 1: *holding the feather*
And nothing else has happened to you lately?

HERMIT:
Well — yes — this happened. I happened to be out in the yard scraping out my frying pan when coming down through the air I saw — a falling star.

It does. It is yellow.

BOY 2:
What are you going to do with this falling star, Mr. Winemeyer?

4. CEMENT SCULPTURES

SCREEN: Actual slides of the Goderich, Ontario, primitive sculptor Laithwaite — his cement figures.

HERMIT:
Come out with me to the orchard and see my latest cement sculptures.

On cue, the sculpture slides appear. They could also be mimed by the Company.

Now here's Sir John A. at the plow!
Here's Snow White and the Seven Dwarfs. That's the only film I've ever seen and the only one I'll ever see. You can't go any higher than that in film art.

BOY 2:
Who's this?

HERMIT:

> That's the infant Riel suckled by the buffalo Manitoba.

BOY 1:

> What's this one doing, Mr. Winemeyer?

HERMIT:

> I finished that last April — that's Mackenzie King
> cultivating the rows of compromise. Now — here is
> where I'm using this falling star. Here's Good —
> in a terrible combat with his brother Evil — over —
> this.

> > *He places the star between the statue-actor's
> > hands. The star has now become a lump of rock.*

BOY 2:

> Could I have a piece of that star?

HERMIT:

> Why sure. These two projecting knobs will never be
> missed. Both have a piece.

BOYS:

> Gee, thank you, Mr. Winemeyer.

> > *We hear music. The Windlady appears with
> > her Rain Doll.*

HERMIT:

> Now there's a good subject for a piece of sculpture.

BOYS:

> What, Mr. Winemeyer?

HERMIT:
> The Wind and the Rain.

> *He and his statues fade slowly. BOY 1 starts*
> *playing the bicycle spokes. BOY 2 goes back*
> *and says:*

BOY 2:
> Mr. Winemeyer — was the pig your brother? Were you
> the peacock?

> *Mr. Winemeyer shakes his head.*

> *SCREEN: Centre panel shows a large star.*

BOY 2:
> What are you doing?

BOY 1:
> I'm kicking this stone into town.

BOY 2:
> Isn't that the piece of a star Mr. Winemeyer gave you?

BOY 1:
> I'm going to see if I can kick it all the way into town.

BOY 2:
> What happened to your bike?

BOY 1:
> Flat tire.

BOY 2:
> Are you going into your music lesson?

BOY 1:

Yep.

BOY 2:

Good luck.

BOY 1 kicks the stone off the stage.

GRAM, as the Music Teacher, comes in and sits down in the chairs arranged for Mr. Winemeyer's hermit hut, but she faces the other way. She plays an invisible piano. Her pupil now enters without the stone.

5. THE MUSIC LESSON

GRAM plays the Teacher, FATHER plays the Pupil.

TEACHER:

That will do for your scales. Now play me your piece. Play me "The Storm." What shall I set the metronome at?

PUPIL:

Set it at summer and pink and white and yellow bricks sunlight with blue sky and white feather dumpling clouds.

The whole Company enter and assist orally:

THE STORM

A cloud and a cloud and a cloud
Came into the blue afternoon room
   A cloud and a cloud and a cloud
   And a cloud and a cloud

a cloud
Mac Leod
A Cloud
And a cloud and a cloud
Down down down came the cloudy
With a windowpane shudder
And mirrors for your feet
People running into stores
Darkness in the library
Umbrellas blossom
Church is nearer through the rain.
A cloud and a cloud and a cloudy
Came out of the yellow garage
Joseph MacLeod in a many-coloured vest
Danced to the Music dying in the west.

The whole piece should have the feeling of yellow and "Chansons sans Paroles" by Mendelssohn.

TEACHER:

Why are you looking so sad?

BOY 1:

I've lost something. I've lost a piece of the star Mr. Winemeyer gave me. I was trying to kick it all the way into town and it disappeared in the dirt.

TEACHER:

Here — as a reward for playing "The Storm" so well.

She hands him the star.

BOY 1:

But Miss Miller. How did you get hold of this? It's my piece of the star . . . that I lost while kicking it into town.

She sits down at the piano and begins to play.

TEACHER:

Now here's the next piece of music I'd like you to learn.

*She plays the same piece the Hermit played —
"On Wings of Song."*

BOY 1:

Miss Miller. Tell me the truth. Are you really Mr. Winemeyer in disguise? Are men and women the same?

*She smiles and continues playing. Fading light.
The Windlady and the Rain Doll pass with
their branch shadows. The Music Teacher
disappears. Crawling onstage comes the Hermit,
Mr. Winemeyer. The BOYS run over to him.*

6. THE DEATH OF MR. WINEMEYER

BOY 1:

What happened to you, Mr. Winemeyer?

BOY 2:

Don't try to move. You're bleeding.

MR. WINEMEYER:

I was on top of the barn and I suddenly knew that if I trusted Him — I could fly like an angel. But it was my own fault — I lost faith and fell down in the yard here. I must have spent all day just crawling past my own henhouse. Oh — before you can fly like a butterfly you must crawl like a worm.

BOY 1:

    I've got my bike. I'll go get a doctor.

MR. WINEMEYER:

    Nothing doing. Help me over to that hollow log there.
    Help me to crawl inside it. It's a magic log the Indians
    made. I found it in the lake. There.

        He disappears into the log. The statues appear.
        Snow falls on them. From the other end of the
        log emerges a huge pale green luna moth. It flies
        away.

BOY 2:

    Come back, Mr. Winemeyer.

BOY 1:

    He's not in the hollow log.

BOY 2:

    I know. Come back. Come back.

        They run off.

        As the stage turns green and in huge letters
        TORONTO, YONGE STREET come on.

FATHER:

    And the rest of my life has been looking for that
    butterfly and that moth. Up Yonge Street. Down
    the Red River. At the Dance of Death.

7. GREEN AND VARIOUS FRAGMENTS

Green suggests Thursday, NOPQ, Jack in the Pulpit, Mars, "Wilson's Hymns," "The Japanese Sandman."

SCREEN: Announces with MOTHER:

MOTHER:
>Green is for Thursday, NOPQ, Jack in the Pulpit, the planet Mars.

>*A transition sequence in which we are reminded that originally this started with a man remembering his life, being initiated into finding some pathway through it, his finding out how many colours and selves he broke up into, his finding out how both hostile and loving the most normal figures in one's life could be.*

>*The Main Characters line up and recite part of the existence poem.*

ALL:
>The pebble is a huge dark hill I must climb
>The pebble is a huge dark hill I must climb
>The dewdrop's a great storm lake you must cross
>The string was a road he could not find
>The straw will be a sign whose meaning they forget
>Hill   Lake   Road   Sign

PA:
>>But the farm-nest tipped
>>>And Father split in two;
>>Uncle Good and Aunt Evil
>>>Took me in, how do you do.

They lived in a House of Day
It had a Yard of Night;
It stood on a street of Puzzle Town
On a refuse graveyard site.

Behind the gasworks Cain got me.
He crushed me like a nettle.
A sweet faced boy named Abel brought me
His dearest treasure, a piece of gravel.

After he died — I went away to live in cities ever since.
Cities like Toronto, Winnipeg, London, Ontario. You
never see anyone you know. I'm walking up Yonge
Street — and miles outside of the city I can see the
Luna Moth — I can see the soul of Mr. Winemeyer
enter the temple at Sharon — miles north of Toronto —
a white temple all made of wood and 12,000 panes of
glass. I can hear them singing.

> SCREEN: A slide of Sharon Temple — 30 miles
> north of Toronto.

CHOIR:

Oh Gilead's joy, where is thy spring
Or healing that thy balm affords?
Oh, where do Zion's children sing,
Or Jesus loose the binding cords.

The David Wilson hymn with barrel organ melody.

> SCREEN: Big sound and image montage of city
> crowd and traffic.

PA:

But I can't get across the city. I can't find my way
out of it. I can't even shut out the noise of the place
so I can hear them singing.

GRAM:

> You've probably committed some crime or other.
> What did you do with the piece of the star Mr.
> Winemeyer gave you?

PA:

> I lost it again. What will help me?

GRAM:

> The first green leaf of love. Watch and don't lose that.

> *SCREEN: Green Leaf appears.*

ALL:

> A TRAIN FROM STRATFORD TO TORONTO
> Shakespeare   New Hamburg   Baden

8. BIBLE SAL ON THE TRAIN
FROM STRATFORD TO TORONTO

> *The station name sequence should go under this
> dialogue. Train effects. The train is made of
> chairs.*

SON:

> Hello, Sally. You going to Toronto too?

SALLY:

> Yes. I'm going to work my way through Bible College.
> And you?

SON:

> I'm going to University College. How's the writer's
> cramp coming?

SALLY:

>You'll lose your faith at that college.

SON:

>I'm hoping to find it. Why don't you come over some time and listen to some of the lectures?

SALLY:

>I'd lose my faith.

>*She has an arm in a sling.*

SON:

>How's the Bible coming these days? Whatever happened to your arm?

SALLY:

>It was copying out the Apocrypha. The Israelites were pretty shaky when I last saw them. The Old Testament — I gave up my right arm to it. I guess, if I ever do, I'll have to write the New Testament with my left.

SON:

>What'll you do if your left hand plays out?

SALLY:

>It probably will — round about Second Corinthians.

SON:

>Maybe your right will be better by that time.

SALLY:

>I used to feel that if my arms gave out I'd write it with my feet. And if I couldn't do that, I'd put the pen in my mouth and I'd write Revelation with the

pen held between my teeth. But I don't know now.
Perhaps it's enough just to do the Old Testament.
I lose heart a bit at times you know. That fire at the
Y.W.C.A. — I had to recopy all of Chronicles and
Kings. You don't get over that in a hurry.

ALL:

Peterloo   Kitchener   Guelph
Rockwood   Georgetown   Limehouse
Brampton   Weston   West Toronto

Union Station crowd hollow murmur.

Parkdale   Union Station

*BOY and SALLY arrive in Toronto and mime a
tour that leads to the college. First they rush
from station to help GRAM who lies grovelling
against the edge of a parking lot.*

SON:

Here — let us help you.

SAL:

What on earth has happened to you, you poor dear.

GRAM:

I've just been attacked, that's what's the matter with
me. Two brutes came out of that beer parlour there
and dragged me in behind this old church.

SAL:

Oh, how terrible.

SON:

What can we do to help you?

GRAM:

> Help me — which way is it — help me to the corner of
> Bay and Shuter street.

SON:

> We — don't know this city very well.

SAL:

> You'll have to direct us.

GRAM: *rising*

> Your first time here, eh?

SON:

> Yes.

GRAM:

> Well — welcome! Welcome to Toronna!

> *Noise. Form a coat-of-arms set-up. GRAMP is*
> *Dexter — an Indian habited proper, within his*
> *boot a scalping knife and in his right hand a*
> *tomahawk with his left arm leaning on a bow.*
> *GRAM is Sinister Britannia helmed and cuirassed,*
> *holding a trident in her right hand and with her*
> *left hand resting on a shield charged with the*
> *union of the three crosses proper. These are*
> *part of Toronto's coat of arms.*

ALL:

> Industry, intelligence, integrity.
> Raw Truth nailed to the screen!
> Sam, Sam the Record Man!
> Ban for sale, Banish Odours
> Chanel No. 5 for Sale!

Traffic symbols, blinking excavation lights,
crossbucks.

ALL:

Gas it! When necking becomes something else!

Screams and traffic noises.

Girl, 17, who wrestles with boyfriend headed for
trouble!

GRAMP: *with megaphone*
Wanted: one capable baby sitter, college student
preferred. No references. Apt. 22B, 1223 College
Street, Thornview Apartments.

SCREEN: Slides of University College and its
gargoyles.

GRAMP: *with megaphone*
And on our left — the quaint old Gothic Victorian
building, University College, University of Toronto.
Outside it is trimmed with one thousand corbels
carved in stone by a Bohemian stone carver. Inside it
is decorated with one thousand corbels carved in
wood by the same old gentleman and no two of them
the same. His *chef d'oeuvre* is admittedly a fantastic
wood gryphon at the bottom of the East Staircase.

SALLY:

I will come with you to a lecture. Perhaps it will
do me good. It's my day off and I'm not due at
Moody Hall until suppertime.

SON:

What's your job, Sally?

SALLY:

I work in the kitchen at the college here.

SON:

This is Dr. Button. Old Testament Studies. I usually go to sleep on all the coats back here.

SALLY:

Old Testament Studies. What a treat!

They sit down with the rest of the Company on the chairs which have been arranged for a lecture room.

9. UNIVERSITY COLLEGE: THE LECTURE OF DR. BUTTON

GIRLS:

Oh, Dr. Button. We came across this tremendous article on Babylonian women in *Mademoiselle.*

BUTTON: *played by GRAMP*

Go away!

BOYS:

Sir. A friend of mine and I have been working on the possible influence of Chinese ideograms on Babylonian cuneiform.

BUTTON:

No influence at all. You're too precocious. You know what precocious means? It means — cooked too soon. All black and burnt on the outside. All running and raw doughy inside.

BOYS & GIRLS:
> Oh, sir.

> *SCREEN: Shows a series of philosophers,*
> *teachers such as Frye and McLuhan.*

BUTTON:
> My lecture for today — Herman Shultz. Finally,
> Gunkel J. Hempel, O. Einfeldt, A. Weiser, A. Bentger.
> Widengren's book falls into two parts Pfeiffer barely
> allows Ezra as an international person. Yahweh.
> Quite naturally I hope that no one in this room believes
> literally all that is in the Bible. The Holy Spirit cannot
> teach you French in two minutes. The sun has never
> stood still. Whales choke on oranges let alone fully
> developed prophets. Yahweh is someone the Israelites
> made up over a period of years during their wanderings —
> very useful, but not really there. Originally Yahweh —
> Jehovah or God to some of you — was probably a
> volcano. A volcano in eruption. Do I meet with any
> opposition to these remarks? I like to have some sort
> of opposition. Let me sketch out the opposing positions.
> One of them might be that there is a holy creative force
> which binds the Universe together, inspires people to
> believe in something — after all a volcano is better
> than nothing. All wrong of course, but I'm surprised
> you back there asleep on all the coats haven't made
> your usual outburst.

SON:
> A flower is like a star.

BUTTON:
> Oachghwkwk! A flower is not like a star! Nothing is
> like anyone else. Anything else. You've got to get
> over thinking things are like other things.

SON:

>Then if a flower is not like a star, and nothing is like
>anything else then — all the spring goes out of me.
>I used to take such pleasure in little things — images,
>stones, pebbles, leaves, grasses, sedges — the grass is
>like a pen, its nib filled with seed — but it all seems —
>lies. I can't go on. There seems no reason to go on
>living or thinking.

BUTTON:

>Surely there are some basic drives that you don't have
>to get all tortured with thought about. Why after
>Mrs. Button has cooked me one of her excellent dinners
>and we retire for an evening of endearments and jollity,
>there seems at least one reason for going on. Have
>another such dinner, another such evening.

SON:

>Are people like each other then?

BUTTON:

>I'm not like Mrs. Button. Otherwise we'd not have
>so much fun.

>*Class laughter.*

SON: *advancing as if to assassinate*
>A flower is like a star!

BUTTON: *advancing too as in a menacing Kabuki scene.*
>Don't come at me like that. A flower is not like a
>star.

SON:

>You're a bear whose paw is over my sun.

BUTTON:

You've served my purpose. Class — that's the imaginative point of view. Give it a big hand, before it falls asleep on your coats again.

Applause

SON:

Don't you believe in anything?

BUTTON: *pause*

Not a thing. Ever since Fritz Schmidlap was caught planting 12th Century shards in a 9th Century dig. Imagine the idiocy of believing anything in the Old Testament. Why there's a girl works in our college kitchens who's not only copying out the whole Bible into Woolworth's scribblers, but believes literally every word it says.

SAL: *rising*

Sir — I am that girl. And I believe in God — or Yahweh as you call him. And I believe every word I possibly can of the book he wrote.

BUTTON: *dry laugh*

I suppose you think he wrote it in English.

SAL:

He knows English for I have prayed to him in that language and he has answered me.

BUTTON:

In English?

SAL: *pause*

How well do you know your Bible — in English, sir?

BUTTON:

>Very well indeed. Last year I was elected President of the Oriental Institute. I am a linguist of no mean renown and world authority on Ugaritic ostraca.

SAL:

>Exodus, Chapter 34, verse 14, says?

BUTTON:

>For thou shalt worship no other god: for the Lord, whose name is Jealous, is a Jealous God. Kings II, Chapter 9, verse 33?

SAL:

>And he said, Throw her down. So they threw her down and some of her blood was sprinkled on the wall and on the horses: and he trode her under foot. Kings II, Chapter 10, verse 26 says?

BUTTON:

>And they brought forth the images out of the house of Baal and burned them. You believe no doubt in the Holy Spirit. Yes?

SAL:

>Yes.

BUTTON:

>And that he or it can give you the power to speak with tongues?

SAL:

>Yes. I believe.

BUTTON:

>Do you, in fact, know any other language but your mother tongue?

She shakes her head.

I thought not. Anyone here know German, Hungarian, French. Yes?

As hands are raised.

You precocious youngsters. I will also test her out in Ancient Babylonian. Ready? I will ask you a question in a foreign tongue. The Holy Spirit will give you the power no doubt to reply to me in that tongue.

SAL: *shutting her eyes.*
 I pray that he will.

ALL:
 French!

BUTTON:
 Moi et toi, ces seuls noms dans mon invocation?

 From Claudel's version of "Electra."

SAL: *hesitantly, then more and more smoothly.*
 C'est à toi de comprendre et de considerer.

ALL: *cheering*
 German!

BUTTON:
 Wo hinaus so früh, Rothkäppchen?

 From Grimm's "Red Riding Hood."

SAL:
 Zur Grossmutter.

The little girl's lines.

BUTTON:
Was tragst du unter der Schurze?

The wolf's lines.

SAL: *lit now in a blaze of glory*
Kuchen und Wein: gestern haben wir gebachen, da
soll sich die Kranke unser schwache Grossmutter et
was zu gut tun, und sich damit starken!

ALL:
Hungarian!

BUTTON:
Hungarian yourself! Ancient Babylonian. I'll get
you and your Holy Ghost there. No Berlitz School
can teach an ignorant kitchen slave Ancient Babylonian.

ALL:
Ancient Babylonian!

*We've let the typewriter wander over the first words
of the Bible.*

BUTTON:
Bresith bara elohim eth kassamayim weth haarec.

SAL:

Whaarec hayatha tho hu wabbobu whoselch alpne
thehim. Weruah marahepheth hammayim wayymen
yehi or YEHI or WAYEHI WAYEHI

*BUTTON exits in shame and wrath. Underneath
the love scene, FATHER and MOTHER chant
over metaphor equations: flower star deer branch
tree antler antler branch clock heart eye sun
mouth bell cloud Greenland*

ALL:

A flower is
like a star!
A flower is like a star!
A flower is like a star!

SCREEN: Star — flower — butterfly — montage.

SON:

No, no. Try this. A flower is a star.

ALL: *chanting in the background*
A flower is a star. A flower is a star.

SON and SAL walk towards each other.

*SCREEN: Green leaf. By this time thy SON
and SAL should be standing on chairs.*

SAL:

Do you remember that great big leaf we found on the
island?

*Sing this à la Les Parapluies de Cherbourg. Let
the actors and pianist make up their own tunes.*

SON:

Yes. Adam and Eve could have hidden all their shame
in it.

SAL:

Have you pressed it for me in the heaviest book in the
library?

SON:

I did. But someone took out the heaviest book. I
can't find out who.

SAL: *spoken*
What a shame! If you had been able to give me the
green or a luna moth leaf . . .

SON:

Teach me how to believe the way you do.

SAL:

My darling . . . isn't it simply that   *she presents*
herself to him, but he turns away   no one can teach
it to you. It teaches you — to itself   *an embrace*
in which he is backward to her   But instead I'll finish
copying out the whole Bible. Tonight — I'll begin
the New Testament. I have the strength at last to
write of Jesus.

10. BLUE — AND SO TO WINNIPEG
AND A FANTASIA ON THE STREET NAMES

Blue suggests Friday, RSTU, chicory, Saturn,
a Doukhobor hymn, Pierre Falcon's "Chanson."

SCREEN and MOTHER announce:

MOTHER:
Blue is for Friday, RSTU, Chicory and the planet
Saturn.

*SCREEN: Frames of cold blue, various pictures
of Winnipeg winter now appear. Train sounds
and chairs being arranged in a long line facing
the audience. The train goes through Northern
Ontario — actually two trains, since Group I says
C.N. and Group II says C.P. stops.*

GROUP I:
  Eagle River
  Gunne
  Pine Hawk Lake
  Keewatin
  Whitemouth
  Sioux Lookout
  Red Lake Road
  Redditt
  Ottermere
  White
  Emma
  WINNIPEG!

GROUP II:
  Vermilion Bay
  Edison
  Scovil
  Kenora
  Shelley
  Julius
  Hudson
  McIntosh
  Farlane
  Minaki
  Winnitoba
  Hector
  Anola
  Portage la Prairie
  Deer
  Cloverleaf
  Hazelbridge
  WINNIPEG!

*This is conducted as a class with each line spoken
by a different scholar.*

*SCREEN: Map of Winnipeg along with street
scenes.*

A FANTASIA ON THE STREET NAMES OF WINNIPEG

for three or more voices

I met a nun coming up Osborne Street
You met an Osborne coming up Fort Street
He met a Portage Fort coming down Main
She carried a Kennedy filled with Dagmar
It, Broadway, balanced its rows of elms
We ate nothing but Pembina all that Wellington Crescent
You Assiniboine far too much about Gertie
They Corydoned their gay Oxfords and Ashes
I beg you Osborne. Portage your Main this conjugation.
To be a city system, Winnipegging the whole thing?
That's exactly what I Main Street South.
For Example:

I Winnipeg	We Winnipegged
You Winnip	You Winnipdown
He Winni	
She Winnipeggied	They Winnipugged
It Winned	

The Past Tense of To Winnipeg?
I'm not sure but I think that it would be —
I Winnipuzzed?

11. THE WRITING CLASS (AND CALLING ROLL)

FATHER:

I have just taken a walk during the break on the
grounds of the Home Economics and Interior Design
Institute in the 40 degree below weather we're having
and I've found something I'll show you later on.
Meanwhile, the roll.

> *This goes under the writing class very softly —
> who face us on the line of chairs, sometimes
> getting up to give us a Winnipeg impression.*

Miss Susan Putlee
Bev Resnick
Cynthia Robertson
Vivian Scrose
Chris Silver
Victor Smith
Marilyn Tretnik
Rudy Waldman
Natalia Walters
Alex Webb
Ann Webb
Marcia Wilder
Sidney Barkley
Doug Brock
Joan Cheyne
Margaret Chiswin
Victor Cleland
Emilia Cosgrove
John Davies
William Danielson
Raymond Danzinger
Robert Dubrokevsky
David Domytrak
Christine Epstein
Donald Greenberg
Wayne Haid
Robert Haynes
Jane Isbister
Henry Klein
Sidney Kuryluk
Arnold Lee
Lintie Lopeck
Ray Lunney

Diane Austin
Alan Bingham
Rae Birchard
John Burrell
Gordon Bowman
Alex Cockle
Maria Diner
Gail DeRosario
Maxine Funk
Nicholas Hershfield
Jerry Ilynsky
Gail Hoeving
Hannah Johnson
Helen Katz
Maurice Kornek
John A. Kraut
Larry Kucin
Linden MacDonald
Gerald Morosnik
Linda Neil
Margaret Paul
David Riddell
Gerald Rigg
Bruce Rosner
Sheila Schwartz
Sam Watson
Raymond Wiebe
Donald Meledszus
Lynne Mindess
David Mirochnik
Dan Moonan
Rita Zelcovich

This goes under the Writing Class and should be endless like a film spool — try to end with Zelcovich when the other sequence splices in.

FATHER:

>All right. You were asked to bring a sentence of two on something or somebody you actually saw in a walk about the city. Let's hear them.

>>*These impressions are spread out among the Cast:*

>I saw some people who lived in a packing box.
>I saw a bundle of rags reach for its Aqua Velva.
>A bundle of rags crouched under a bridge.
>The Franklin gulls flew over the wharf.
>I saw the fairytale castle by the river.
>I saw a mother, a mother and father not much bigger than their five children.
>We saw people looking at the ice breaking up in the river.
>Winter leaves the city today.

>>*Train whistle.*

>Just inside the old station I heard one young loiterer say to another:
>"Do you know . . . when I do it once . . . I can't do it again that day again. You know?"
>A Bouncing rhyme — when spring comes to the grimy coal dust streets round the Red River grain mills near Lorette Street in the Sunset, kids with long shadows sing:
>>And what did you do there sir.
>>I caught a polar bear sir.
>>How many did you catch, sir.
>>One, sir. Two, sir. Three, sir, Four, etc.
>I saw a man (father?) daughter? son? which of them perhaps her husband walking on the dike along the river.

The young man said pointing down at the rusty tangle
   in the river mud: "That's my cat! That's my cat —
   this is where I drowned it last winter." "Yes. Yes.
   Oh is it?"
"This is a nice walk. We must remember to take it
   again. Why did we never think of it before?"
At sunset, as the darkness gathers in the small park
   by the river . . .

   A man suddenly leaps high into the air.

"You don't know what it's like. The
   old time poetry. You don't know what it's like."
"I don't know."
"But I say you don't know what the old time poetry
   is like."

FATHER: *calls*
   . . . Rita Zelcovich

   One of the group replies drowsily:

Present.

FATHER:
   Yes. Now — see what I found during my walk in the
   snow just before the lecture. Underneath the scrub
   oaks by the river and the alder thickets — a dead bird.
   An indigo bunting. Total blue. On the snow. Do you
   know who it is? It's the body of someone slowly
   freezing to death — frozen to death with the hard
   heart and deaf ear that will not listen.

ALL:
   Is the dead bird you? Do we have to listen.

FATHER:
    It's you. It's me.

12. THE MESSENGER – RECITATION

FATHER:

THE MESSENGER

Over the plain and under the sky
    The signposts whirl like weathervanes
The sun guesses where his shadow to throw
    The four hooves crash the puddle ice panes.

He draws the mountain to him
    He fattens the distant speck
Away I've no time for you, he says;
    He scampers the lake and the beck.

The forest he shovels past
    Dark branch cannot hold him
The geese expand in the village
    The chimneys and steeples brim:

He says – in the market place
    To windows and faces and crowns
Eyes and keyholes and dogs
    Sides and tops, ups and downs.

Leave the burning city
    Leave this burning town
Destruction cometh – a sucking cloud
    Your towers will tumble down,
        Eaton's & The Bay.

But this city is not burning,
    A wise old idiot says,
And there's no war we've heard of:
    The young matrons titter & gaze.

The messenger beats his brow
    The stupid pavement ups
The ignorant gables close him in,
    The streetplan him cups.

Till the Babylon becomes him,
    The city disappears,
And over the plain & under the sky
    He gallops with truthful fear.

Leave this burning city!
    Will no one listen to me?
Even now the doomfist knocks
    It's the sound of our hearts, say we.

ALL:

Over the plain and under the sky
Over the plain and under the sky
Over the plain and under the sky
Over the plain and under the sky.

13. COCKTAIL PARTY

A CROWD IN WINNIPEG

Done as a cocktail party — in the background we hear snatches of a Doukhobor hymn.

VOICE 1:

Miss Handlebar and Mr. Steering Wheel,
Master Accelerator
Were in the crowd as well as all these others
In between Eaton's and The Bay.

MUSIC VOICE:
>
> Mr. and Mrs. Pushbutton, Mr. and Mrs. Eggbeater and Little Miss Weasel.

VOICE 3:
>
> Mr. Mould, Mr. Coffin, Miss Casket, Mr. Embalmer, Mr. Funeral Home, Miss Undertook.

VOICE 1:
>
> Master Window, Mr. Box, Old Mrs. Coconut, Granny Plague.

> *Introductions!*

VOICE 2:
>
> Miss Light, Mr. Short, Miss Belly.

VOICE 3:
>
> Young Cigarette, Old Bum.

VOICE 1:
>
> Mr. Dim Radio, Miss Ghastly Hollow, the Lieutenant Governor.

VOICE 2:
>
> Television Mouth, a dwarf, Miss Idiot.

VOICE 3:
>
> Professor Twaddle, Doctor Horror.

VOICE 1:
>
> Assistant Professor Sulky and Mother Neurosis.

VOICE 2:
>
> Some Hutterites with geese under their arms, Father Monster.

VOICE 3:

And the Sliver girls: Little Sliver, Just as little Sliver,
Sliver.

VOICE 1:

Old Spit, Young Kleenex and 25 Albanians were
in the crowd as well as all these others in between
Eaton's and The Bay.

COMPANY:

The poem breaks in with its different feeling

Pebble dew drop piece of string straw

The string is a road that I cannot find

The straw is a sign whose meaning I forget

What was it that quite changed the scene
So desert faded into meadow green?
The answer is that he met a Tiger
The answer is that he met a Balloon,
A Prostitute of Snow, A Gorgeous Salesman
As well as a company of others such as
Sly Tod, Reverend Jones, Kitty Cradle and so on.

14. BOARDING HOUSE

The chairs are rearranged to give the impression
of a boarding house dining room. Throughout
FATHER has a newspaper which hides his face.
NIECE can be the maid. People change from
one character to another with great speed.
Basically, two tables are presented — and their
conversations.

GRAMP:

I wonder if you've ever read a book called Houseboat
on the Styx.

GRAM:

No. I was back in Germany in 1937. In a cafe I quite
naturally you know lit a cigarette after my meal was
over and I was approached by several who reminded
me that in the New Germany women did not smoke.
Do you know what I said to them?

GRAMP:

It's about a number of famous people gathered
together in a houseboat on the Styx. The River of
Death you know.

GRAM:

Proudly I said. Ich bin eine Canadianische frau.
Ah yes. That stumped them. Ich bin eine
Canadianische frau. And I continued smoking —
Ich bin eine Canadianische frau.

The maid comes to everyone with the menu card.

ALL:

Monday, January 8, 1950.

Clear Soup
Chicken Pie
Boiled Potatoes
Asparagus
Pineapple Upside Down Cake
Beverage

SON:

I'm not so fond of Chicken Pie.

GIRL: *played by MOTHER*
Why? Is it very strange?

SON:

Well — it has hardboiled eggs cooked in it. I think that's going too far. Sort of cooking the child with the mother you know.

GIRL: *to maid*
No Chicken Pie for me, please.

SON:

Just the potatoes and asparagus, please.

The soup is brought in.

Change chairs and tables to suggest different sets of people.

MOTHER:

In 1901 my sisters, brothers and I went to hear Mrs. Pankhurst speak at the harbour. At Douglas, in the Isle of Man, you know.

109

FATHER:

And how did you like that?

MOTHER:

Oh we didn't like it at all. My brothers had water pistols. They rowed out in a boat and aimed them at her. My sisters and I laughed and laughed.

FATHER:

Mrs. Pankhurst couldn't convince you about female suffrage, could she?

MOTHER:

No. Never. Although I have voted you know. When an excellent candidate appears for our party in our riding.

FATHER:

And you just sat by while your brothers soaked the woman who got you the vote — your political rights?

MOTHER:

No, no. The war did you know. And my sisters and I didn't just sit by. No indeed. My sister threw six rotten eggs at Mrs. Pankhurst. And I got her with a large decaying turnip I found at the bottom of our garden. She fell into the water and very nearly drowned. I thought we would kill ourselves laughing.

SON:

Why has Mrs. Selver got no tail?

NIECE:

Why.

SON:

> She comes from the Isle of Man?

NIECE:

> Explain.

SON:

> Manx cats? They haven't got any tails, have they?

MA: *in a tougher more waspish version.*
> What were you doing in his room so late last night?

GIRL: *played by GRAM*
> None of your business, Mrs. Whiter.

MA:

> Everything under a roof that was once mine is my business. Why aren't you eating your bacon, Paul?

SON:

> There's something in it.

MA:

> A piece of steel wool. By golly we could all have been poisoned. Steel wool could just cut your stomach lining to pieces.   *to maid.*   Tell the cook woman to come out here. I want to talk to her. She's in love with you, Paul. She wants to kill you.

GIRL:

> I praise steel wool. It got her off us. My her ears are sharp.

SON:

> Nothing worth hearing either. Just quietly playing chess.

GIRL: *played by MOTHER again*
Mr. Clockwinder had a heart attack last night. Right in his masonic apron.

GRAM: *changing character, coming to SON*
This was my boarding house. I founded it because there was no place in Winnipeg you could have tea with a correct table setting. My father was a vicar in Devonshire. There were thirteen of us in our family. Holly in the lane. Tell me — when I died why did you refuse to be one of my pall bearers?

MAID:
The cook says she won't come out. She says she spent ten years in Stoney Mountain for knifing a woman just like you.

FATHER:
She loves you, mother. She wants to knife you.

MA:
I've got my column on the Story of how our favorite hymns come to be written typed out for fifteen years ahead.

SON: *to GRAM*
I don't know why. I couldn't face it. I was sick. I can't even face your chicken pie.

ALL:
Who was the Tiger? Christ.
Who was the Balloon? Buddha.
Emily Brontë and the Emperor Solomon.
Who sang of his foot in the doorway.
All these met him. They were hopeful and faithful.

15. YONGE STREET — A DENUNCIATION OF TORONTO

PA: *assisted by the others*

" " *indicates a group chant or another voice.*

I curse this street where it's increasingly difficult to
    find a green leaf.
I curse Yonge Street.
Existence waked me here on this cement tapeworm
    "This one day and every day"
And if you did not eat, expect some trouble
From the angels on the bridge in the golden dray.
"I curse the discovery of fire. I curse Prometheus."
It has more or less — step upon step, breath after breath
    "This one day and every day"
And if you did not dream, what will they say
At the narrow gate in the wall around the orchard.

I can remember the tokens that more or less made it all go;
It was more or less Queen Elizabeth's face in your pocket.
I can remember a fish's skeleton at Savarin's Restaurant
The crowds of other-me's walked above the rush
Lakeward of their own defecation and urination
"Where is the golden wand and branch we lent you?"
A Melinda St. boss ate it like a candy stick,
Cement-suited he had bellies under his eyes.
"Where is the silver cup and grail we gave you?"
A King St. woman with installments for eyes,
Typewriters for feet and spare tires for hair
    "This one day and every day"
        pawned it.

SON:

"Your camera factories are getting so big
There's nothing left to take pictures of but camera factories"

113

PA:

    But I have here this long grey vertebrae
    The backbone of Toronto; my backbone too.
    Cars and street dust and plate glass and something
    That's my journey and my life.
    If it got nowhere
      This one day of all the days
        Nowhere's somewhere.

16. THE FABLE OF THE BABYSITTER AND THE BABY

    *The Cast change into a family in a crowded
    Toronto apartment.*

GRAMP: *with megaphone*
    Wanted: one capable babysitter, college student
    preferred. No references. Ap. 22B, 1224 College
    St., Thornview Apartments.

VOICES:
    Glad you've come. Ah — the babysitter. Glad you've
    come. *ad lib repetitions*

PA:
    Where's the baby? Has he gone to sleep yet?

    *The "baby" is behind a sheet screen so that we
    see the latter part of this scene in silhouette or —
    no screen. Just the SON with his shirt off
    — back to the audience, sitting on the floor.*

VOICES OF PARENTS, RELATIVES, ETC.:
    Over there. Over there behind that curtain. *ad lib.*

    They disappear.

The baby played by the SON walks out and squats
with his naked back to the audience in Centre Stage.
He bunches in his arms so that he looks deformed.

PA:

You're not a baby. You're a fully grown man.
Why didn't they — Oh my God, what's the matter
with you.

SON:

I haven't got any arms — nor any legs. I wasn't born
with any. I'm just a torso — lying here in bed. Every
half hour you should turn me over to my other side.

PA:

I'm not going to stay with you.

Stepping out from behind the imaginary screen.

They should have told me.

SON:

Please don't leave me. I cannot be left alone for too
long. I don't need your physical help so much.
Remember —no one told me I'd be put inside this
hollow trunk without any flippers or grabbers. You're
walking up Yonge Street. I'm walking up Yonge Street
too with left breath, right breath, left breath, right
breath, breath in, breath out. I need your love.

PA:

I have no love to spare. I can't bear sickness and pain
in myself or others. I reject completely all the messy
ways we sail coffins in our seed. Don't you curse your
parents' lust?

SON:

> I'll curse them if they brought me into a world where
> a student at the university cannot even turn a pillow
> for a godforsaken flat on his back, no arms, no legs
> monstrosity. I want you to read something to me.
> And I have to be cleaned again.

PA:

> I can't read to you. Why can't I see?

SON:

> Because you're holding your hands over your eyes.

PA:

> What should I read to you? I could read it on this
> side of the curtain.

SON:

> Ranch Romances. There's a whole pile of them on the
> chair there. Too vulgar for you, eh? And you'll have
> to come closer — behind the curtain.

> *SCREEN: The Green Leaf appears — framed*
> *in purple.*

PA:

> Ranch Romances. *opening up one* Where did
> this leaf come from? It's the leaf Sally and I found
> on the island.

SON:

> Things you've lost are inside things you don't like.

116

PA: *turning slowly back*
> Yes. I love you. Without feet you walk with your
> breath. Without hands your body is a giant's hand.
> I love you.

17. WEDDING

*The Babysitter scene fades away. We hear the
Sharon hymn. The BIBLE GIRL hands FATHER
a model of Sharon Temple — the building he
longed to enter when he felt trapped in cities,
the temple he saw Mr. Winemeyer's luna moth
soul entering. Now he's struggled with Yonge
Street sufficiently well to deserve Sharon.
CHILDREN bring forth a wedding arch.*

ALL:
> Who was the Tiger: Christ
> Who was the Balloon?   Buddha
> Emily Brontë and the Emperor Solomon
> All these met him. They were hopeful and faithful.

The family tree pyramid has formed.

TO GROW UP

Needs	Evidently
One thousand and 24	dirty handkerchiefs
Five hundred and 12	pimples and boils
256	irregular French verbs
128	failures to rise on time
64	library fines
32	visits to the dentist
16	just plain failures
8	attempts
4	almosts

       2   eyes
       1   successful Act of Love

Everyone is dressed for a wedding — might be photo-
graphed any time. After MOTHER and FATHER
kiss under the arch. All the CHILDREN come
out between them — in large mother-and-father-
heads like those worn a way back in the Berry
Picking scene. All these children are produced
by love; they are mothers and fathers and so on.
But there is a change as blue shades into purple.
CHILDREN come through now in Hallowe'en
masks and carrying a coffin with the quilt in it
used by Grandmother and Grandfather in the
first Red sequence about the Ancestral Bed.

18. PURPLE

Suggests Saturday, VWXY, Wild Aster, Hallowe'en,
Jupiter.

SCREEN: Announces with MOTHER:

MOTHER:
    Purple is for Saturday, Wild Aster, VWXY and the
    planet Jupiter. Hallowe'en.

One of the SINGERS announces:

The Dance of Death at London, Ontario

GRAM and GRAMP in death masks conduct a
Danse Macabre with the actors.

GRAM & GRAMP:
>Blow the trumpet! Beat the drum!
>>This town's a dance of death.
>Did you think you could not come?
>>You'll dance when you're out of breath.

>*In the centre of the stage GRAMP swings*
>*MOTHER, FATHER, SON and NIECE around*
>*as if on strings. GRAM with slapstick keeps*
>*the dancers on their toes, and herds them*
>*round when the time comes to say their part.*

>*SCREEN: in centre screen the King of Death.*

>Executive Esquire & Grocery Boy
>Man, Woman, Doctor, Child, Bishop
>The Scavenger & the Rich Young Lady
>Painter & Poet & Cop

>*MOTHER, FATHER, NIECE and SON take*
>*various parts. The music used is a macabre*
>*version of the first Dance of Life music at the*
>*birthday party. The SINGERS announce each*
>*title.*

19. THE DANCE OF DEATH

THE EXECUTIVE

I walk back from the club to the office
Though Queens Avenue knows the weight of my Rolls Royce.
>Life Insurance ensures my assurance.
At this moment five girls type my voice.

>*The Executive collapses and goes limp; so do they*
>*all the moment Death begins to speak.*

DEATH

Hey! Where do you think you're going?
I need you to type out my deeds.
  I've a nice tidy room where you'll work
Though the ribbon is tangled with weeds

PRIEST:

THE CLERGYMAN

I often think as I drink tea
Of Faith and Hope and Charity

MINISTER:

  I'm sure that Faith, Hope and Charity
Oft think of us as we drink tea.

DEATH

Shepherds, the morning sky is red
I've found half of thy charge.
Whatever thy task was, find it out,
  For I'm near and much at large.

THE RICH YOUNG LADY

My father breaks hundreds of bonds
  My mother subscribes to The Queen
I spent last winter in Antigua
  Our swimming pool's drinkably clean.

DEATH

Then come ride with me and my hounds
  Or if you wish to this car keep,
And we'll drive with the speed of the wind
  To my park where the shadows are deep.

SHE:

THE BRIDE AND THE GROOM

Mother and Father have spared no expense.
Is that someone's foot on my train

HE:

I bet I remember this moment
Again and again and again.

DEATH

There go the bride and the bridegroom!
They'll stay at our hostelry.
To its luscious bridal chamber
We've devised an ancient key.

THE GROCERY BOY

At the corner of Richmond and Talbot Street,
Oranges, cornflakes, cellophane and ham,
I fill up the bags and the boxes.
Is that black car the one you mean, M'am?

DEATH

Long enough have you drudged for the stomach!
Drop that box at your feet in this parking lot!
It's just dust that I need for my supper.
Put yourself in this box that I've got.

*Death and his Queen lead off his victims
in a ragged line. He cracks the line of them
like a whip. They are his slaves and disappear
into his country.*

20. THE LIGHTNING ROD:
IN WHICH THE CHILDREN AGAIN TRIUMPH
OVER SCHOOLMASTER DEATH

> *But as his music fades, from the back of the*
> *auditorium march the CHILDREN. The*
> *CHILDREN of the company now arrive.*
> *One of them carries a white flag with a cross*
> *on it. Toy trumpets are blown.*

> *SCREEN: A child fights a skeleton. The Dance*
> *of Death stops. They bear a baby in a cradle.*

CHILDREN: *when they reach centre stage*
This is the last living baby left in the whole world.
The rest of us are now ghosts. There may be a few
other babies, but no one knows where they are hidden.

DEATH LADY: *with a rat in a cage*
I'll send a rat to gnaw this baby up.

CHILDREN:
The baby sleeps peacefully. Unless he wakes up
and cries, his parents will not come with him before
the rat's poisonous teeth sink into his heart.

DEATH KING:
Well — wake him up then. Rat — I'll let you out of
this cage.

CHILDREN:
He can't bear our voices. Long ago we all died.

> *The CHILDREN start raising a high lightning rod.*

DEATH LADY:
Here — what are they doing that for?

Use step ladder.

DEATH KING:
> There's a storm in the air tonight. If they attract the thunder here with their lightning fishing rod — the brat may wake up and call for his Mother and Father. Crouch down or the lightning and thunder may come at us. Put that lightning rod down.

> *He pulls it down. A tug of war.*

> Let the Rat loose.

CHILDREN:
> We've got a fox will eat up your rat.

DEATH KING:
> Let loose our dog. It will chase away the fox and eat the baby.

CHILDREN:
> We've got a stick. It beats your dog away.

DEATH KING:
> Keep that down. Fire. Use fire.

CHILDREN:
> Water — water. Put out the fire.

DEATH LADY:
> Ox — ox. Send our ox to drink up the water — then give the child to death.

CHILDREN:
> My uncle, the butcher, will kill your ox.

Draw this out because it is the uncle, the butcher's strength that saves the baby.

DEATH KING: *forgetting to keep hold of the lightning rod after a fight*   Well, I'll fix him.

In mime he slays the butcher, but meanwhile the lightning rod is raised. Lightning and thunder awaken the baby. Its cries bring in the parents, at the sight of whom the Death King and the Death Lady cower away.

Trumpets

SCREEN: Child triumphs over Death. Then no images.

21. BLACK AND RECOVERY

Black suggests Some Day, Omega, Indian Pipes, Z, the Earth.

Back at the opening Birthday Party.

MOTHER: *quietly*
Black is for OMEGA, Some Day, Indian Pipes, The Earth, Z.

Then the light comes up to reveal the sick child of the first scene sitting in a chair, his eyes bandaged.

KID:
But mother — I am better. Can the bandage be taken off so I can see?

MOTHER:

 Here's a cup of water. Why yes. I think your eyes
 can bear the light now. My poor child — you almost
 died on us several times.

 As she unwraps the bandage.

KID:

 I haven't seen the light for 40 days, mother, have I.
 I've watched colours in the dark. I've thought of so
 much that has been and is and will be, I guess. Red
 and Yellow and Blue things. Purple things. Black
 things.

MOTHER:

 Now — I'm about to unfasten the last fold.

ALL:

 Hill   Lake   Road   Sign
 But love and patience do quite change the scene.

 Now the mountain becomes   a pebble in my hand
 The lake calms down   to a dewdrop in a flower
 The weary road   is string around your wrist
 The mysterious sign   is a straw that whistles
                              "home"

 Pebble   dewdrop   piece of string   straw

KID:

 Mother, when I got sick, it was still winter and
 everything was covered with snow. But the Spring
 came.

 SCREEN: Colours in the Dark

125

MOTHER:

The Spring has come and you didn't know.

KID:

And the grass is green. The branches are covered with leaves.

ALL:

1024 great great great great great great great great grandparents
512 great great great great great great great grandparents
256 great great great great great great grandparents
128 great great great great great grandparents
64 great great great great grandparents
32 great great great grandparents
16 great great grandparents
8 great grandparents
4 grandparents
2 parents
One child.

GIFTS

Existence gives to me
What does he give to me
He gives to me   a pebble
He gives to me   a dewdrop
He gives to me   a piece of string
He gives to me   a straw
Pebble dewdrop piece of string straw

The pebble is a huge dark hill I must climb
The dewdrop is a great storm lake that we must cross
The string is a road that I cannot find
The straw is a sign whose meaning I forget
Hill   lake   road   sign

What was it that quite changed the scene
So desert faded into meadow green?
The answer is that he met a Tiger
The answer is that he met a Balloon,
A Prostitute of Snow, a Gorgeous Salesman
As well as a company of others such as
Sly Tod, Reverend Jones, Kitty Cradle and so on

Who was the Tiger? Christ
Who was the Balloon? Buddha
Emily Brontë and the Emperor Solomon
Who sang of his foot in the doorway.
All these met him. They were hopeful and faithful.

But love and patience do quite change the scene
Now the mountain becomes a pebble in my hand
The lake calms down   to a dewdrop in a flower
The weary road   is a string around your wrist
The mysterious sign   is a straw that whistles home
Pebble   dewdrop   piece of string   straw